STOCK INVESTING FOR YOUNG ADULTS SIMPLIFIED

DISCOVER HOW TO EVALUATE STOCKS, MANAGE RISKS, & BUILD A WINNING INVESTMENT STRATEGY

RAMAN KEANE

CONTENTS

INTRODUCTION

Everyone seems to have an opinion on investing. Some people love it and swear by it, while others shy away from it and tell you horror stories about how this one person they know has a brother who has a friend who has a cousin who lost all their money through investing. Most of us believe these stories and cling to them, using them as an excuse not to educate ourselves about investing and the stock market. We shy away from the possibilities and prefer to use these stories as a crutch to justify our unwillingness to invest.

Although the awful story we all heard might be true, chances are the brother's friend's cousin probably lacked a bit of knowledge on the investment front, which is why they lost all their money. Or they simply didn't take the necessary steps to mitigate their risk, like diversifying their portfolio. Whatever happened has a reason behind it and a way they could have avoided losing everything.

The risk is always there, but the more you know, the more vigilant and thorough you will be and the smaller the chances of losing everything. Actually, if you gain the right knowledge and apply it effectively, you could even become a multimillionaire.

Did you know that one of the wealthiest people in the world bought his first stock at the age of 11? When I was 11, the only thing I thought about was what my mom packed for lunch, who I was going to hang out with during break time, and whether my parents would buy me a see-through ruler that was impossible to break. My mind was nowhere near buying my first stock.

Back to the story. Although his father was a stockbroker, he had an interest in making money from a young age and made it his business to find out everything he could about making money by investing. Over the years, he has been a beacon of hope to those in the investment industry. His roots started in investments, but he is a well-known businessman who inspires millions across the world.

Were you able to guess who it is? I'll give you a hint: One of his famous quotes (also referred to as a pearl of wisdom) states, "If you aren't willing to hold a stock for 10 years, don't even think about holding it for 10 minutes." (Dolan, 2024).

It is none other than Warren Buffett, of course.

I know what you're thinking: Warren Buffett's case is quite unique and extreme. It's true that not everyone will reach Warren Buffett's level of success, but that doesn't mean success isn't within reach for everyone.

Many investors begin small with a specific focus, like dividend-paying stocks, and gradually diversify as they gain more knowledge. By attending seminars, watching videos, and reading extensively about investing, they develop the skills needed to make informed decisions. The biggest tip is to start small and keep learning as you go.

Just because you haven't started yet doesn't mean you've missed your opportunity. It's never too late (or too early) to start. The focus should be on taking the first step and building wealth through smart and consistent investments.

Starting earlier does have its perks, though. The younger one can get into the stock market and invest, the better. By starting young, you reap the following benefits:

- You can take more risks: Younger people can take more risks with their investment choices because they have more time to recover from possible losses. Higher risks can lead to greater rewards when approached correctly. As you grow older and near retirement, you should start moving away from risky investments and take a more moderate or conservative approach.
- You have more time to grow your investments: The longer you can invest money, the more interest you will earn. That's the beauty of compound interest. So, the sooner you start, the bigger your investment will grow. We cover some of the basics of investing in Chapter 1, which includes the concept of compound interest.
- You build up experience: Many of us learn by doing. When we make a mistake, we learn from it so that we can avoid it. Okay, maybe sometimes we need to make it a few times before we avoid it, but you get what I mean. When you're young, that is the time to build up

experience and learn from mistakes so you can become old and wealthy with years of knowledge and experience. By making mistakes while still young, you give yourself enough time to recover and recoup some of the money you've lost.

- You have more to invest: Most young people have more disposable income than the older generation simply because they don't have as much responsibility (or haven't had the opportunity to rack up a mountain of debt). This means that they have more money to invest. You don't need millions to make millions. You need a small seed that can turn into millions over time.

- Cultivating healthy habits: People are more likely to continue investing when they're older and make a success out of it if they start young. This is because they learned from a young age to put money aside for investing and use their years of knowledge to know how to invest. Building healthy financial habits is easier done when you are still young because you have more time to dedicate to it. As you grow older, you take on more responsibility, and honestly, your energy levels and willingness to learn something new tend to decrease. Cultivating these healthy financial habits while you're young helps to set you up for the future.

If these benefits don't entice you to start investing, I hope that the thought of growing your money exponentially and retiring comfortably will do the trick. It's okay if you're not quite sure what you're doing yet. In this book, we will go through the process step by step together.

According to Solá (2024), approximately 63% of young adults feel that the stock market is the answer to building wealth; however, very few actually do it. And I had to ask myself the question: Why? If they know it's a really good place to invest, why are they hesitant about doing so?

I don't believe there is a single answer here. There could be a few reasons why young adults are not comfortable with investing in stocks.

One of the big reasons might be the skewed perception that has been created concerning investing and the stock market. I'm not saying that risks don't exist. However, the perception has been created from a point of ignorance. So many people have made a success out of investing that I can't believe the stigma that it's too risky and the possibility of losing it all is bigger than gaining wealth. Yes, the stock market is volatile and can seem complex and difficult to understand, but with the right financial knowledge, it's a breeze to navigate.

Investing in the stock market is a good way to increase your money and start saving for retirement. Although normal savings accounts are not bad, the interest rates are substantially lower, you don't get regular payouts, and the money grows a lot slower than it would with stock market investments. We all know that the cost of living increases year by year, and it has almost become essential to find alternative means of income along with some investments for the future.

Another issue I often come across when speaking to young adults is the reliability of the advice they are receiving. Some people just give bad advice. If the person hasn't made a ton of money through investments but believes this will be their big break, it's best to take their advice with a grain of salt and do your own research. Not everyone who is passionate about giving financial advice has the authority to give it. If you want sound financial advice, it's best to consult with a financial advisor.

In saying that, it's important to mention that I am not a certified advisor, and the contents of this book should not be regarded as financial advice. The book contains knowledge to help you understand investments better and know how to navigate investments. For any financial advice, it's best to consult a professional.

This book has been specifically written for young adults who are new to investing. It still covers all the important concepts and is filled with pearls of wisdom that will help any young investor to start on the right foot, with simplified explanations and using everyday language. No need to worry about crazy jargon. Wherever I use financial jargon (only when it's appropriate and important), a detailed definition or explanation is included.

By working meticulously through this book, you will:

- Feel empowered through financial education.
- Receive practical, actionable advice.
- Learn effective risk management.
- Be in a position to achieve long-term financial growth.
- Feel more confident and independent.

This book contains a structured step-by-step approach to stock investing that simplifies complex concepts, like understanding key financial metrics, developing a personalized investment strategy, managing risks effectively, and building a balanced portfolio. This will help empower you to make confident, informed decisions.

Imagine being the friend or family member that has it all figured out. The one who is financially stable, confident, and independent with more than enough investments to carry them through a difficult time (and retirement one day). Smart investing helps us create the life we want.

Are you ready to take the first step to a better, financially independent life? Let's get started.

1

THE BASICS

There is nowhere better to start than with the basics. In this chapter, we will cover the fundamental concepts of stock investing, such as what stocks are, how the stock market functions, and the inherent risks and rewards involved. These concepts are pivotal to understanding the advanced topics covered in subsequent chapters. If you think you already have a good understanding of these concepts, I encourage you to still work through the chapter as a refresher that will also ensure that you understand the content to follow in the subsequent chapters.

To kick off the discussion and deep-dive into investing and the stock market, consider the journey of Peter Lynch, who became one of the most successful mutual fund managers by focusing on understanding the basics. Starting as an intern, he eventually managed the Magellan Fund, achieving an average annual return of 29.2% from 1977 to 1990 (Chen, 2024d). Lynch's success was built on a deep understanding of stocks and the market's workings.

Understanding and mastering the basics is what separates someone who struggles with stock investing from someone who builds a successful future through it.

What Is a Stock?

A stock is basically a share in a company. The word "share" means a unit of stock. When you buy stocks of a specific company, you share in the ownership of the company.

You can obtain shares through stock exchanges (also referred to as stock markets). In the next section, we will explore what exactly they are and how they work.

When you own a stock, you have certain rights associated with it. The rights or privileges that you have as a shareholder depend on the type of share you buy. Depending on the type of share, you may have some (or all) of the following benefits:

- **Dividends:** The payments that companies give shareholders based on their profits. Directors are in charge of deciding what percentage of the company's profit can be paid as dividends. These payments are made regularly and can become an additional source of income.
- **Inspect corporate documents:** As a shareholder, the company is obligated to share certain documents with you, such as minutes of board meetings and the company bylaws. Financial reports should be available

to the public and be periodically reviewed by shareholders, specifically the annual report and Form 10-K. We will discuss financial statements and what to look for in Chapter 2.

- **Ownership:** The value of your share changes when a company performs better or worse. The value can increase, meaning that your shares are worth a lot more down the line than they were when you bought them. Although your overall ownership doesn't increase, the value of your ownership does. Keep in mind that it can also decrease if the company starts performing poorly. Keeping an eye on the financial statements and understanding the company's plan of action when they face adversity will help you make an informed decision if the need arises.

- **Transfer of ownership:** Depending on the goal you wish to achieve, you can choose to either hold on to the shares or sell them once they reach a certain value. This is referred to as transferring ownership and is done through a stock market. Due to the liquidity of stocks, it's generally quite easy to transfer ownership when you decide to let go of your shares. You are not obligated to hold on to a stock for any specific amount of time, but be careful not to over-trad. We discuss this concept in Chapter 8.

- **Sue for wrongful acts:** Shareholders generally have the right to access and review financial information and are allowed to sue the company if they suspect any suspicious activity, such as overstating earnings or hiding true financials from shareholders. Companies may see this as the only way to keep shareholders invested, which is why it's essential for shareholders to review the financial statements and annual reports as soon as they become available and question any irregularities.

- **Voting rights:** As a shareholder of a common stock, you will have voting rights to elect or appoint directors and vote on any proposals that may affect the company's financial situation.

Common Versus *Preferred Stocks*

Investors typically focus on two main stock types: common and preferred.

A common stock is what we described at the beginning of this section. It represents partial ownership in a company and provides access to specific financial information and corporate documentation. Owning a common stock also allows you to vote at shareholders' meetings.

A preferred stock shares some features with bonds. A bond is a type of fixed-income asset where you lend money to a company or the government in return for interest over a period of time. Although this sounds great, it comes with its own set of risks, challenges, and cons—the biggest being that you have no voting privileges.

Table 1.1 illustrates the main differences between common and preferred stocks:

	Common Stocks	**Preferred Stocks**
Dividends	The dividend payouts can differ based on the profitability of the company.	The dividends are fixed, regardless of profitability.
Voting rights	Shareholders have voting rights.	Shareholders don't have voting rights.
Claim to earnings	Shareholders are paid after preferred stockholders.	Shareholders are paid before common stockholders.

Table 1.1 Common stocks vs Preferred stocks

Understanding Stock Markets

The stock market is where investors trade stocks, and companies raise capital by issuing them. Any public company can list shares and other securities on the stock market to be traded. Most stocks are traded through stock exchanges. In addition to stock exchanges, there are over-the-counter (OTC) marketplaces. Here, investors can trade securities directly among one another without going through a stock exchange. In this book, we'll mostly focus on the stock market.

Brief History of Stock Markets

To gain a proper understanding of something, it's always a good idea to start with the history of it.

The European stock market dates back to the 13th century, while the U.S. stock market only became part of the economy around the 18th century. After hundreds of years, we've definitely learned a few tricks of the trade (Hwang, 2024).

The first company to trade publicly was the Dutch East India Company, and in 1611, the first stock exchange was created in Amsterdam. A few years after this, more and more companies started trading shares and paying their investors dividends. There was great excitement among investors, which resulted in emotional investing, and some made mistakes, buying shares without researching the company and thoroughly analyzing their financial statements. In 1720, one of the earliest major financial bubbles burst, causing widespread losses among investors (*History*, n.d.).

Although it might be the first major time investors lost money, it definitely wasn't the last time. Something that is clear is that investors always get back to it. However, we learn from our mistakes and make better decisions the next time. The stock market's volatility and being afraid of it is not a new concept. Keeping that in mind, imagine if everyone decided back in 1720 that it was too risky. We wouldn't have a stock market to trade on today. The stock market has changed investing for the better. Yes, there are risks, but the bigger the risk, the better the reward. This will become clear as you go through the contents of this book. Back to history.

The Philadelphia Stock Exchange, founded in 1790, holds the distinction of being the first stock market in the United States. Additionally, a group known as the Buttonwood Traders convened regularly to facilitate stock trading, leading to the establishment of the Buttonwood Tree Agreement. This agreement ultimately evolved into what we recognize today as the New York Stock Exchange (NYSE). Initially, this exchange operated as a physical venue with a strict dress code, requiring members to purchase a seat for participation. Isn't that fascinating? (Hwang, 2024).

In contrast, the National Association of Securities Dealers Automated Quotations (NASDAQ), another prominent U.S. stock exchange, was established in 1971. Approximately eleven years later, it pioneered the first intercontinental securities market through a partnership with the International Stock Exchange in London. NASDAQ was also the first platform to enable electronic stock trading for investors (Hwang, 2024).

How They Operate

Stock markets consist of individual shares of companies as well as indexes, like the S&P 500 and Dow Jones Industrial Average. These indexes are collections of shares from different companies. The performance of the entire index is a good indication of how the companies within that index are doing, so you don't need to keep track of the companies individually.

While "stock market" and "stock exchange" are often used synonymously, they refer to distinct concepts. The stock market uses stock exchanges to operate. There is one stock market but multiple stock exchanges.

In the United States, there are two main stock exchanges: the National Association of Securities Dealers Automated Quotations (NASDAQ) and the New York Stock Exchange (NYSE).

Companies use these stock exchanges to list their shares using a process called initial public offering (IPO). These initial shares are purchased by interested investors, and the company uses the money to grow the company. In exchange, investors get access to specific information and may have voting rights depending on the type of stock, as discussed earlier. Once the shares are owned by an investor, the shares can be traded among investors if they don't wish to keep them.

Investors can list their shares at an asking price on the stock exchange, and anyone interested can bid on the share. There is usually a difference between the two, and this is referred to as the bid-ask spread. The bid and ask price need to match before a trade can occur, so either the seller needs to reduce their asking price or the buyer needs to increase their bid.

Factors That Influence Stock Prices

By understanding what influences the stock market, investors can better manage their investments and anticipate when to make changes. Let's explore some of the most common factors that influence stock prices.

- **Supply and demand**: One of the primary influences on stock prices is this factor. It's not a new concept, and you probably deal with it daily in various aspects of your life.
  - Simply put, supply and demand refer to how much there is of something and how that translates to the need in the community. If there is a need and scarcity, something is much more valuable. So, if the supply doesn't meet the demand, then the price increases.
  - If everyone starts selling a particular stock, then the supply goes up, and prices go down, and vice versa.
- **Industry trends and sector performance**: Any advancements or changes within a certain industry (such as technological advancements) affect stock market prices for that industry or sector.
- **Inflation**: This has a direct impact on disposable income; with inflation, people tend to have less

disposable income to invest. Fewer investors mean the demand is lower with ample supply.

- **Market speculation, news, and trading activity**: The power of the media is often underestimated. Speculation regarding the market can influence stock market prices as more and more investors trade on a specific index or stock. Although these may be short-term fluctuations, they still affect the market.
- **Natural calamities**: Any natural disasters or calamities, including pandemics and epidemics, can affect the stock market prices.
- **Political and regulatory factors**: Stock markets are quite sensitive to various political factors, such as a weak government, uncertain political situations, war breaking out (or the possibility thereof), elections, etc.

Investing *Versus* Speculating

Have you ever heard the phrase "Past performance does not guarantee future results"? The Securities and Exchange Commission (SEC) obligates investment firms to say this to protect themselves in case past performance does not live up to expectations in the future.

However, what are you then supposed to base your decision to invest on? Does that mean that by investing, you are speculating that it may go well? Although it might seem that way, investing and speculating are two completely different concepts, and you can invest without speculating. Avoid falling into the trap of basing your future investments on speculation alone.

Let's examine the two concepts more closely and discuss what to focus on to ensure that your choices are based on investing and not speculation.

Investing can be defined as a long-term strategy for building wealth over time. There is no space for a "get-rich-quick" mindset. When investing, one doesn't focus on the price of the shares but rather on the company's performance. Although the price is important to consider, as you don't want to purchase overpriced shares, it shouldn't be the only measurement you use to make your decision. We cover the concept of overpriced and undervalued shares later in the book.

Speculating leans more toward short-term trading and focuses on making as much profit as possible in very little time. There is a lot more risk here, but with high risk comes high reward.

To explain the concept a little more, I have included Table 1.2 with the differences.

Although it might be tempting to chase after profits in the short term, the risk that comes along with it is not always worth it. Most people who lose all their money in what they call investing actually speculate in the hopes that they can get value for money now. When they lose their money, they blame investing and shy away from it for the rest of their lives.

Speculating is not the only pitfall when it comes to investing, and we discuss these in detail in Chapter 8.

By focusing on long-term strategies and investing your money, there is less risk with a steady growth in wealth. What's even better is the fact that you can use compound interest to your advantage to make your money work for you. What is compound interest? I'm glad you asked.

	Investing	Speculating
Definition	A long-term strategy with the intention to build wealth over time.	Short-term trading for quick profits.
Time horizon	Long-term.	Short-term.
Level of risk	Moderate risk.	High risk.
Returns expectations	Slow and continuous growth of funds over time.	High rate of return in a short time; however, losses are experienced just as quickly.
Decision criteria	Always consider fundamental factors, like the current performance of the sector and/or company.	Based more on opinion, market influence, and technical charts.
Investor attitude	They are mostly cautious, do their homework, and are conservative when investing.	They like to take risks but can be labeled as careless.
Examples	Real estate, bonds, high-quality stocks, and annuities.	Some of the Penny stocks and cryptocurrencies.

Table 1.2 Investing vs speculating

The Eighth Wonder of the World

Compound interest was famously called the "eighth wonder of the world" by Albert Einstein. Understanding compound interest is important, not only for investments but for overall financial literacy. The truth is, if you don't understand how compound interest works, you're more likely to pay it—through debt—than to earn it and grow your wealth.

Compound interest is interest calculated not only on the original principal but also on the accumulated interest. Trust me, once you grasp it, you'll never forget. Think of compound interest as a snowball. You start with a small snowball. If you let the snowball roll down a hill, it picks up more and more snow and exponentially grows into a much bigger snowball.

That's exactly what compound interest is and how it works. If you invest a small amount of money with compound interest, you will earn interest on the initial amount. The next time interest is added, it's added based on the initial amount plus the interest already earned. When you invest (or save) with simple interest, interest is only earned on the initial principal amount without taking the interest gained into account.

Let's look at an example where we compare simple interest with compound interest.

If you start with an initial investment of $500 with an annual simple interest rate of 5% over 20 years, with no additional deposits, your investment could look something like this:

- After the first year: $500 + 5% of $500 ($25) = $525
- After the second year: $525 + 5% of $500 ($25) = $550
- After the third year: $550 + 5% of $500 ($25) = $575
- After the 10th year: $725 + 5% of $500 ($25) = $750
- After the 20th year: $975 + 5% of $500 ($25) = $1,000
- So, after 20 years, the total interest earned would be $500 in simple interest.

If we now use the same initial amount of $500 with an annual compound interest rate of 5% over 20 years, with no additional deposits, the picture looks a little different:

- After the first year: $500 + 5% of $500 ($25) = $525
- After the second year: $525 + 5% of $525 ($26.25) = $551.25
- After the third year: $551.25 + 5% of $551.25 ($27.56) = $578.81
- After the 10th year: $775.66 + 5% of $775.66 ($38.78) = $814.45
- After the 20th year: $1,263.48 + 5% of $1,263.48 ($63.17) = $1,326.65
- So, after 20 years, the total interest earned would be $826.65. That's a difference of $326.65.
- If you invest for up to 30 years, you will earn $750 in simple interest and $1,660.97 in compound interest.

To really take advantage of compound interest, it's important to invest as early as possible and keep the investments for as long as possible. Compound interest is one of the main reasons why you should start investing as early as you can. The smallest investment can grow into a big nest egg over time.

Some of the world's most wealthy people, like Warren Buffet, love compound interest and advocate for it every chance they get. They didn't get rich overnight. It took years of patience and the power of compound interest to get and maintain their wealth.

When you know how to take advantage of compound interest, you can invest and forget about it. You don't need to check on it multiple times a day. This doesn't mean that you shouldn't still check your portfolio regularly. It's essential to ensure you're still meeting your goals, but we'll go into more detail on that in Chapter 7.

Of course, compound interest has a negative side as well. It becomes our worst enemy when we get into debt. However, this book doesn't focus on that aspect, but it's an important fact to be aware of.

Where There Is Investment, There Is Risk

Risk exists everywhere. We are faced with risks every day of our lives. Any decision that we make comes with risks, and we base our choices on whether the reward we will gain is worth it. Some people are willing to take more risks, and others are more conservative.

It's not always easy to navigate this because the only way we know whether something is worth the risk is by looking back on our own experiences or other people's stories. If you don't have any experience nor know of anyone who was faced with something similar, it's difficult to calculate whether it would be worth it. The same can be said when it comes to investing.

There will always be inherent risk when investing, regardless of the type of investment you choose. Investments that have a lower risk tend to come with lower profitability (or a lower chance of appreciating), but there are still risks involved. One of the most fundamental parts of investing is knowing how to manage the risks.

We can define Investment risk as the probability of losing money due to any factor that may influence the price. There are different types of risks, which we discuss briefly below. It's important to understand these risks so that you know how to manage them.

- **Concentration risk**: When we put all our eggs in one basket, we are faced with concentration risk. This means that if the value depreciates for that specific stock, the investor loses most (if not all) of their money. We run into this risk when we choose a single asset, stock, or industry to invest in. If something goes wrong and that stock or industry suddenly crashes, we lose everything.
- **Credit risk**: This can also be referred to as default risk and refers to the possibility that a bond issuer (this could be a government or a company) might not be able to meet its financial obligations. These financial obligations include paying interest or repaying the principal when the bond matures. This risk is tied to the financial health of the issuer.
- **Horizon risk**: There is always a risk that something will happen in life that will shorten the investment horizon, forcing the investor to let go of the investment earlier than expected. This includes loss of a job, sudden illness, or any other emergency where money is needed urgently.
- **Inflation risk**: When inflation outpaces investment returns, your gains lose purchasing power, creating inflation risk. For example, if you buy a bond at a 3% interest rate and the inflation rate increases to 5%, your real return is -2%.
- **Liquidity risk**: This risk refers to the difficulty of selling an asset quickly without significantly lowering its price. You may find it difficult to sell some stocks or investments, potentially resulting in a lower sale price than anticipated or, in extreme cases, an inability to sell them.

- **Longevity risk**: This is the risk of running out of money during retirement, i.e., you outlive the savings accumulated. This is why planning for retirement from a young age is vital.
- **Market risk**: This relates to the danger of an investment declining in value due to economic influences, specifically equity risk (the risk of stock prices falling), currency risk (the risk of exchange rate fluctuations for investments in foreign currencies), and interest rate risk.
- **Reinvestment risk**: This is the possibility that when you reinvest the earnings (like interest payments) from an investment, you might have to accept lower returns because interest rates have dropped. This risk applies if you rely on regular payments and need to reinvest them at the current lower rates, which could reduce your overall returns.

Managing Risks

Here are three ways to manage risk:

- **Be consistent**: It's better to invest small amounts regularly than only invest when it looks good. Decide on investment intervals and be consistent. Invest the same amount at the same intervals. This will help to average out the investment and provide some security with any possible volatility. Dollar-cost averaging is a great example of this. We discuss this method a little later in the book.
- **Be *in it* for the long term**: We spoke about speculating and investing. Make sure that you are

always in it for the investing, which means you invest long-term. The longer you invest, the more the investment will yield.

- **Diversify**: Diversification is one of the most important factors when it comes to investing. Having a diverse portfolio means that your investments are not made up of only one type of investment. Look for different sectors or industries to invest in and invest in various assets. Although we're focusing on stocks in this book, it's good to broaden your horizons and look into other assets, such as bonds and cash investments. We'll touch on this in more detail later.

Let's take a look at a diverse portfolio example containing different types of assets. The exact percentage of each asset will depend on the individual, but this example illustrates the types of assets that might be included.

The idea is to create a portfolio that's balanced so it handles market ups and downs, grows consistently, and is diversified to lower risk. We will cover these aspects and how to create a diversified portfolio in the chapters to come.

I have included a brief description of each asset as well as an explanation to support why this type of asset is important to include in a diversified portfolio.

- Stocks: approximately 50% of the portfolio
  - International stocks (10%): These are shares of international origin, such as Asian or European equities. It helps to balance a portfolio by tapping into other economies that may be unaffected by changes in the U.S. market.

- Small-cap stocks (10%): These are shares of smaller companies that may offer higher growth potential. The only downside is that they may be more volatile than larger companies.
- U.S. large-cap stocks (30%): These shares are for large and established U.S. companies, such as those on the S&P 500 index. They tend to be stable and have long-term growth potential.
- Stocks should make up the largest portion of most portfolios because they are the most growth-orientated asset. Diversifying across large, international, and small markets helps to reduce risk.
- Bonds: approximately 30% of the portfolio
  - U.S. Treasury bonds (15%): One of the safest investments is U.S. treasury bonds. These bonds are backed by the government. It's a very stable investment, and you receive regular income through interest.
  - Corporate bonds (10%): These are bonds from established companies. Although still considered quite safe and low-risk investments, they tend to provide higher returns than government bonds.
  - Municipal bonds (5%): These tend to be tax-free bonds issued by state or local governments.
  - Bonds provide a predictable income stream to balance out the ups and downs of stocks. By also diversifying the types of bonds (government, corporate, and municipal bonds), you manage risk and generate a moderate income.
- Real estate investment trusts (REITs): approximately 10% of the portfolio

- You don't have to own property to invest in real estate. By investing in REITs, you can add real estate to your portfolio without the responsibility of maintaining a property. We don't discuss REITs in this book, but it's important to note that this could be part of your portfolio. REITs offer regular dividends and add more diversity as real estate performs differently from stocks and bonds.
  - By including real estate, you add a potential hedge against inflation to your portfolio. It's quite stable and provides income.
- Cash and cash equivalents: approximately 10% of the portfolio
  - High-yield savings account (5%): This type of savings account accumulates the most interest out of all the savings accounts. You're able to access funds whenever you need.
  - Money market funds (5%): These are short-term and low-risk investments with high liquidity. You're able to access funds relatively quickly.
  - You need cash investments to ensure you have funds available for emergencies or immediate opportunities without the need to sell any assets.

This type of portfolio works because the diversified structure reduces the investment risk by spreading investments across asset types that perform differently. This means that when the one goes down, the others are likely to go up or remain constant. Stocks provide growth, bonds add the stability required, REITs may help hedge against inflation, and cash investments ensure liquidity. Balancing these assets in a portfolio aligns with a long-term strategy and supports and protects against market fluctuations.

Chapter Summary

Understanding the basics of stock investing and possible risks is pivotal before you can move on to actual investing.

- Companies list shares on the stock market, which is managed through stock exchanges. Investors who buy shares have ownership in the company. By owning shares, they may have certain rights:
  - Access to dividends.
  - They can inspect corporate documents.
  - They have part ownership.
  - They can transfer ownership.
  - They can take legal action against the company for deceitful practices, such as concealing financial realities.
  - They have voting rights.
- There are two different types of stocks: common and preferred stocks.
  - Common stocks are stocks that we all know. Owners of common stocks may receive dividends based on the company's profitability; they have voting rights and are paid after preferred stockholders.
  - Preferred stocks possess characteristics akin to fixed-income securities (bonds). Holders of preferred stocks receive predetermined dividend payments, lack voting privileges, and are

prioritized over common shareholders in the distribution of assets.

- Stock exchanges facilitate the trading of stocks in the stock market. Stock markets comprise indexes, which are a collection of shares from different companies.
- Many factors can influence stock prices, including supply and demand, industry trends and sector performance, inflation, market speculation and trading activity, natural calamities, and political and regulatory factors.
- Investing and speculating is not the same thing. Investing is for the long term, carries a lower risk, and decisions are based on fundamental investing factors. Speculating is for the short term in the hopes of making money quickly. The risk is very high, and decisions are made on a whim based on personal opinion and market speculation.
- Compound interest is something that can make your investments grow, requiring little ongoing effort from you after the initial setup.
- Risk is inherent to any investment. There are different types of risks, and although all may not be applicable all the time, one or more may always exist.
- Successful investing requires understanding and managing potential risks.
- Some ways that we can manage risks are by investing consistently, having a diverse portfolio, and investing long-term.

I know this may have been a lot to take in, but now that we have covered the basics, we can get to the exciting part. In the next chapter, you will learn how to assess a company's financial health and viability as an investment by understanding key financial metrics, balance sheets, income statements, competitive advantages, and management quality.

EVALUATING A BUSINESS FOR INVESTMENT

One of the most difficult decisions to make when it comes to buying stocks is to know which companies to invest in. There are so many options, and everyone has their own opinion. The best advice I can give is to do your research before jumping into something. This chapter will help you to analyze the details to determine whether it would be a good investment or not.

A company that always seems to be at the top is Apple Inc. It comes as no surprise that they have dominated the tech industry for years by consistently demonstrating strong financial health and competitive advantage. I won't go into the details of why they are so successful, but at a high level, it's because they know what their consumers need. They focus on the *why* instead of the *what* (which is to make money and be successful) (Cook, 2024a,b).

Their ability to innovate and dominate ensures high-profit margins, which is why they are one of the favorites among investors. Apple Inc. is not the only company that can do this, and it's important to understand the factors that make Apple successful in order to identify similar investment opportunities.

Let's explore some key terms that you should understand. We'll learn how to read balance sheets and income statements, how to assess a company's competitive advantage, and why management quality is important.

Key Financial Metrics

Before we get into the nitty-gritty, it's important to go over some definitions.

- **Revenue**: This can be defined as the total income generated from a company's business activities. To determine net income, you use the revenue and subtract any costs from it. A company can have more than one type of revenue. For example, a car company might have a revenue per type of vehicle. You also get accrued and deferred revenue:
  - Accrued revenue is money that a customer still needs to pay for goods or services, i.e., they have purchased the product or service, but no payment has been made yet.
  - Deferred revenue refers to funds received from a customer before the delivery of goods or the provision of services. This revenue will only be acknowledged and documented once the goods are delivered or the services are completed.

- **Profit margin:** This is the percentage of revenue that is turned into profit. This is always expressed as a percentage of the total revenue (above) after all costs have been deducted. If the profit margin is expressed as 20%, this means that for every dollar the company receives in revenue, $0.20 is profit. There are three types of profit margins that we should be aware of.
  - Gross profit margin is determined by deducting the cost of goods sold from the total revenue, expressed as a percentage.
  - Operating profit margin is determined by deducting the cost of goods sold and the operating expenses from the total revenue and then dividing that value by the revenue, expressed as a percentage.
  - You can calculate the net profit margin by subtracting all expenses—including taxes and interest—from the total revenue and then dividing the result by the revenue.
- **Cash Flow:** This is a company's liquidity measure, indicating financial health. It's the inflows (cash in) and outflows (cash out) of a company. To calculate the cash flow, you deduct the total cash outflow from the total cash inflow. This should be a positive value. A negative value indicates that a company is spending more money than it is receiving.

In addition to understanding these terms, there are some important financial ratios that you should take into account before investing in a company's stock.

Earnings per Share (EPS)

This ratio offers insight into a company's profitability. When you invest in a company, you're essentially buying into the future losses or profits of the company. Understanding the profitability is vital to ensure you get a good return on investment.

To calculate earnings per share, divide net income by the weighted average of outstanding common shares.

EPS = [Net income - Preferred dividends] / Weighted average number of common shares outstanding

The higher the EPS, the better. A higher ratio indicates high profitability.

Price-To-Earnings (P/E) Ratio

An important ratio to consider when looking at stocks is the P/E ratio. This ratio mirrors how much investors are willing to pay per one dollar of a company's earnings. A higher P/E may indicate expectations of future growth, but it should be analyzed alongside other metrics to assess actual growth potential.

To determine the P/E ratio, you can divide the current stock price by the EPS:

P/E ratio = [current stock price] / [Earning Per Share]

Earnings per share are calculated using information from the income statement but are typically provided on stock research websites for convenience.

Quick Ratio

This is often referred to as the acid test and measures a company's liquidity by evaluating its ability to meet short-term oblig-ations using liquid assets, excluding inventory.

This ratio omits inventory, offering a more stringent assessment of liquidity and indicating whether a company can fulfill its short-term financial commitments without depending on its stock.

Quick ratio = (Current assets - inventory) / current liabilities

If the ratio is below 1, it indicates that the company may struggle to meet all its obligations without selling some items from its inventory.

If the ratio is one or more, the company has good short-term liquidity and is likely in a strong position to meet immediate obligations.

Working Capital Ratio

This ratio also gives you an indication of a company's liquidity. This indicates whether a company has enough short-term assets to address its short-term liabilities, but it doesn't guar-antee survival as it doesn't factor in how quickly assets can be liquidated or the timing of liabilities.

This is very similar to the quick ratio; however, with this calcu-lation, all assets are taken into account (including inventory).

The working capital ratio can be calculated as follows:

Working capital ratio = current assets / current liabilities

If the ratio is below 1, it indicates that the company may struggle to meet all its obligations. The lower the number, the less likely they will meet obligations. A ratio of 1 means the company's current assets are just enough to cover its liabilities, but it's not an ideal position as it leaves no room for unforeseen expenses.

If the ratio is above 1, the company is likely in a good liquidity position, but its ability to survive a crisis also depends on cash flow and other financial factors. Companies with a balanced working capital ratio are less likely to experience cash flow problems, which reduces risk for investors. However, an excessively high ratio may suggest inefficiency in using resources.

Debt-To-Equity (D/E) Ratio

The D/E ratio of a company represents how much debt a company uses to finance its operations compared to money invested by shareholders (also referred to as equity).

You can calculate the D/E ratio by dividing the total debt by the total equity:

D/E ratio: total debt / total equity

This is important because the ratio can tell you how risky it is to invest in the company. Companies with a high ratio are more risky because they have more debt and a lot more they need to pay back. A low ratio represents a company that relies more on equities to keep its operations running and tends to be at lower risk.

Return on Equity (ROE)

ROE (expressed as a percentage) is a measure of profitability. It represents how well a company is using shareholder's money to grow the company and make a profit.

Calculating the ROE may seem complex, but it's quite simple. ROE is calculated by dividing the net income (after expenses, taxes, and preferred-share dividends but before common-share dividends) by shareholders' equity (total equity excluding preferred equity).

ROE = net income / total equity

A higher ROE generally indicates better profitability, but it should be evaluated against industry averages and other financial metrics to avoid misinterpretation. Normally, an ROE above 10% is considered to be good.

Remember that you don't necessarily need to memorize these formulas, as there are many analytic websites that provide this information for you. The goal is to make these metrics feel familiar to you so they don't seem foreign when you see them.

Financial Statements

Financial statements are essential documents for investors, providing critical information to help them make informed decisions. However, they should be considered alongside other factors like market trends and industry conditions. It's like a dashboard for a company and contains important metrics.

When reviewing financial statements, you're able to analyze key financial data pertaining to the company, such as losses, profits, expenses, and debt. The ability to read and analyze financial statements will save you a lot of time and energy when researching companies. It's a skill every investor should have. This is where you find everything you need to calculate and assess the ratios we discussed.

There are three primary components of financial statements:

cash flow statement, balance sheet, and income statement. Some companies also provide a statement of changes in equity.

Cash Flow Statements

Cash flow statements detail the inflows and outflows of cash in three main categories: operating activities (e.g., day-to-day business expenses and revenues), investing activities (e.g., purchasing or selling assets), and financing activities (e.g., borrowing or repaying debt and issuing stock). Public companies are required to include a cash flow statement in their financial reports. However, smaller private companies may not always prepare one unless needed for specific purposes.

Balance Sheets

This sheet provides a detailed view of the company's financial position at a specific moment, including all assets, liabilities, and equity. Equity, the company's assets, and liabilities are some of the numbers you will find on the balance sheet.

- Equity is the net worth of the company.
- Liabilities are obligations or debts the company owes, such as accounts payable, long-term debt, and accrued expenses.
- Assets are everything the company owns or controls that has value, including cash, inventory, equipment, and investments. It can also include amounts that the company is still waiting for, i.e., payments waiting to come in.

Equity is equal to the assets of the company minus the liabilities of the company.

A balance sheet is easy to read because the headings are quite clear. It includes a section for assets, liabilities, and equity. When reviewing the balance sheet, you can calculate the working capital ratio, quick ratio, and D/E ratio.

Description	30-Sep-23	30-Sep-22
ASSETS		
Current assets		
Cash and cash equivalents	$20 million	$18 million
Marketable securities	$10 million	$9 million
Accounts receivable (Net)	$15 million	$14 million
Inventory	$7 million	$5 million
Other current assets	$5 million	$4 million
Total current assets	$57 million	$50 million
Non-current assets		
Property, plant, and equipment (Net)	$30 million	$28 million
Other non-current assets	$20 million	$19 million
Total non-current assets	$50 million	$47 million
Total assets	$107 million	$97 million
LIABILITIES		
Current liabilities		
Accounts payable	$20 million	$22 million
Other current liabilities	$15 million	$14 million
Total current liabilities	$35 million	$36 million
Non-current liabilities		
Term debt	$25 million	$27 million
Other non-current liabilities	$15 million	$14 million
Total non-current liabilities	$40 million	$41 million
Total liabilities	$75 million	$77 million
EQUITY		
Shareholders' equity		
Common stock	$15 million	$12 million
Retained earnings	$17 million	$10 million
Total shareholders' equity	$32 million	$22 million
Total liabilities and shareholders' equity	$107 million	$99 million

Table 2.1 A sample balance sheet.

Example

Here is a mock example that I created (Table 2.1). This is not a real company's balance sheet, but it works well as a demonstration.

Using this example, let's determine the relevant ratios and provide some insight on these ratios, using the data for 30 September 2023:

- Working capital ratio: current assets / current liabilities
    - $57 million / $35 million = 1.6
    - This is a good ratio, and the company is in a good financial position to cover their current liabilities with their current assets.
    - If we use the data for 30 September 2022, the working capital ratio is 1.38. This shows that the company had a better year in 2023.
- Quick ratio: (current assets - inventory) / current liabilities
    - ($57 million - $7 million) / $35 million = 1.4
    - The ratio is still above one, indicating that the company is in a good financial position to cover liabilities without selling inventory.
- D/E ratio: total debt / total equity
    - $75 million / $32 million = 2.34
    - This means that for every $1 of equity, the company has $2.34 of debt. Whether this is good or bad depends on the industry, what growth stage the company is in, and the rest of the company's financials.

Income Statements

Income statements give you insight into the company's revenue, net profit, and expenses. The income statement and the number of outstanding shares provide the data needed to calculate EPS. It is also known as a profit and loss statement.

An income statement has a few sections that you need to pay attention to.

- The revenue is what the company earned for that period.
- COGS is the cost of goods sold. In a nutshell, it's how much it costs the company to create the product or deliver the service. This includes the materials, labor, utilities, travel costs, etc. For a healthy company, COGS should typically be lower than revenue, but the ideal ratio varies by industry.
- To determine gross profit, subtract the cost of goods sold (COGS) from the revenue: gross profit = revenue - COGS. However, it may already be calculated on the income statement. This is important because it shows how profitable the product or service of the company is when excluding the cost to generate it.
- Another value that should be on the income statement is the operating expenses, which excludes COGS. This is what it costs the company to keep running on a day-to-day basis.
- The last important value is the net profit, which is revenue minus all expenses, including COGS, operating expenses, taxes, and interest. This is important to know because even if the product or

service is profitable (i.e., gross profit looks good), the company as a whole may not be profitable.

You can calculate the following ratios using the income statement:

- Gross profit margin = (revenue - COGS) / revenue
- Operating profit margin = operating profit / revenue (expressed as a percentage)
  - Operating profit = revenue - (COGS + operating expenses)
- Net profit margin = net income / revenue (expressed as a percentage)
  - Net income = revenue - total expenses

Below is an example of an income statement (Table 2.2). Again, this is just a mock statement and not from a real company.

Let's do the same for the income statement and determine the relevant ratios over 12 months.

- Gross profit margin = (revenue - COGS) / revenue
  - They already included the gross profit in the statement, but let's calculate it anyway.
  - ($260 million - $140 million) / $260 million = 0.46
  - Expressed as a percentage, this is 46%. Whether this is a good gross profit margin or not is based on several factors, including the industry and business type. It may be considered good for retail but below average for a service-based business.
- Operating profit margin = (revenue - (COGS + operating expenses)) / revenue

- ($260 million - ($140 million + $36 million)) / $260 million = 0.32
  - Having an operating profit margin of 32% is generally considered strong in most industries.
- Net profit margin = net income / revenue
  - $70.4 million / $260 million = 0.27
  - A 27% net profit margin is considered good because, for every dollar the company makes, it retains 27 cents as profit.

Additional Insights

In addition to these ratios, there are a few other conclusions we can make using these two sheets that would be helpful in determining whether investing would be beneficial (Table 2.3).

Description	Over three months	Over 12 months
Net sales		
Products	$50 million	$200 million
Services	$15 million	$60 million
Total net sales	$65 million	$260 million
COGS		
Products	$30 million	$120 million
Services	$5 million	$20 million
Total COGS	$35 million	$140 million
Gross profit	$30 million	$120 million
Operating expenses		
Research and development	$5 million	$20 million
Selling, general, and administrative	$4 million	$16 million
Total operating expenses	$9 million	$36 million
Operating income	$21 million	$84 million
Other income	$100,000	$400,000
Income before taxes	$21.1 million	$84.4 million
Provision for income taxes	$3,5 million	$14 million
Net income	$17.6 million	$70.4 million

Table 2.2 A sample Income statement.

Category	Key figures	Analysis
Profitability	Gross profit: $120 million Net income: $70 million	Indicates strong profit-ability, efficient cost control, and solid earnings
Revenue growth	Total net sales: $260 million Product sales: $200 million Services: $60 million	The company shows stability as sales are diversified between products and services
Liquidity	Cash and equivalents: $20 million Current assets: $57 million Current liabilities: $35 million	The company can sufficiently cover short-term liabilities
Shareholders' equity	Total equity: $32 million Retained earnings: $17 million	The increase in equity and retained earnings from 2022 to 2023 shows value creation for shareholders
Cash flow	Net income: $70.4 million	Suggests strong earnings potential. However, a detailed cash flow statement is needed to confirm whether cash flow is positive after considering all operating, investing, and financing activities.

Table 2.3 Additional insights from the Income statement and balance sheet.

Assessing a Company's Competitive Advantage

A company has a competitive advantage when they are able to create a product or deliver a service at a lower price or higher quality than their competitors, resulting in them being the company of choice. It's the reason why customers choose one brand over the other.

There are three main areas where a company can have a competitive advantage:

- **Cost**: Delivering a product or service efficiently, allowing for competitive pricing or higher profit margins.
- **Differentiation**: The products or services are superior in terms of either the features offered customer service, or quality thereof.
- **Specialization**: This type of differentiation means that a company is focused on a specific target market, and its products and/or services are specifically tailored to that target market.

If we look at Apple Inc., which we've been using as inspiration, their competitive advantage includes brand development, product design and quality, and customer experience. They excel in all these aspects, and their customers love them for it. They are not the most affordable, but they offer premium quality and a strong customer experience, which many customers see as worth the price (PenMypaper, n.d.).

Types of Competitive Advantage

There are a few different types of competitive advantage, and as an investor, it's important that you know about them. By being able to identify the type of advantage a company has over its competitors, you can determine whether the company is doing enough to keep its competitive advantage or whether there is a possibility that it can be snatched away in an instant, leaving you open to risk.

Let's look at some of the most common competitive advantages with examples of companies doing it right.

Cost Leadership Advantage

This is all about the cost of products and/or services. Companies with a cost advantage manage to keep costs lower than their competitors while maintaining quality. It's easy to offer goods and services at a reduced cost. The tricky part is trying to find a way to do it without compromising on quality, which is not something everyone manages to do.

It needs to also be sustainable. What I've seen happen is companies trying to gain a competitive cost advantage by cutting their prices for the sake of a cheaper product and/or service, and a few months down the line, they have to nearly double the price to keep up with the cost of producing the products or delivering the service. This huge price jump is more detrimental to the customer base than having a sustainable price from the beginning.

A great example here includes the different grocery stores. Most of them give you the same quality products (or acceptable quality), but there will always be one that is a little cheaper than the others. The larger grocery stores are more likely to offer discounted products than the local small grocery store on the corner. This has to do with the larger grocery stores receiving discounts when bulk purchasing. A small grocery store can't afford to bulk purchase unless they have the surety that the produce will sell out before it goes bad.

Walmart is an excellent case study. Although they offer their products at a reduced cost, they still prioritize efficiency and manage to keep a healthy profit margin.

Customer Service Advantage

A company with this advantage strives for customer satisfaction and will do almost anything to ensure it. Higher customer satisfaction may lead to a higher volume of repeat customers, and word of mouth will ensure that new customers come their way.

A focus on customer service includes faster response times, exceptional after-sales service, and superior support before, during, and after a purchase—anything to delight the customer.

Amazon and Apple are both companies with a customer service advantage.

Differentiation Advantage

This is more focused on offering a product or service that is of superior quality, offers additional or novel features, or any other distinct feature that differentiates the company from its competitors (like a brand image). Offering it at a lower cost is not a factor here. Most of the time, anything from companies with a differentiation competitive advantage is more expensive than their competitors. However, the differentiation is worth the price to customers.

An example of this is Apple. We've briefly touched on this already. They offer a wide variety of high-quality products, and although they can be pricey, other companies struggle to compete with them.

Focus Advantage

Companies that aim for this advantage focus on a specific target market instead of a broad audience. Their products or services zone in on a specific audience, and although they may seem restrictive, they can appeal better to their selected customer base. Those customers almost exclusively use that company for all their needs and rarely need to turn anywhere else. The company ensures customer satisfaction and constant cash inflow by catering to their customers' every need.

One example that comes to mind is Nikon, which produces equipment and instruments involving precision optics. This appeals to a very specific audience.

Geographic Advantage

It's all about the location. Having a geographic advantage means that a company is located strategically and in close proximity to customers, resources, or suppliers. This means that they have easier access to those things versus their competitors, who may not be as lucky.

An example here could be a fast-food vendor on or very close to a University Campus or a coffee shop next to a train station. Walmart is also a good example here. Their stores are strategically placed in remote areas to cater to the small towns as well, where the only other option may be the local corner grocery store.

Innovation Advantage

Companies that are great at innovating are always ahead of the curve. They're usually the first to successfully launch new products and services. Many companies try something new, but it doesn't work because the idea either hasn't been thought through (i.e., taking into account the customer journey and everything that goes along with it) or the market is not ready for it. For example, releasing products specifically for the metaverse now might not be widely profitable, as the technology and market demand are still in their infancy.

When done right, this advantage can ensure that a company is always a trailblazer, leaving other companies behind. People are always looking at them to see what is next and trending.

A company that does this really well is Tesla. They have completely changed the game when it comes to the automotive industry, and companies are still struggling to catch up.

Speed Advantage

This one seems pretty obvious. A speed advantage simply means that the company is able to deliver faster than its competitors. Whether it's producing goods, rendering services, importing, etc., they tend to get it done a lot quicker than others.

In a world of instant gratification, this is an amazing advantage to have as long as it doesn't compromise the quality.

One example that we can add here is Amazon. They have amazing turn-around times for delivering once you order, provided that they have the items in stock.

Identifying the Competitive Advantage

When a company has a competitive advantage, it must keep working at it and developing new ways to keep it. It has become increasingly difficult with the advances in technology and customers being more vocal about what is and isn't acceptable, but a lot of companies have managed to keep their competitive advantage by listening to what the people want and staying ahead of the curve.

Some ways you can use to identify some of the lesser-known companies' competitive advantages include:

- **Customer reviews**: What customers love about a company can be a clear sign of its competitive advantage. By looking at customer reviews, you will also have an idea of where the company may be struggling and how that shows up on its financial statements.
- **Market analysis**: It's important to look at the competitors in the same industry. Doing a market analysis will show you the differences and highlight what each company does really well. Jot down what helps the company succeed, what their potential pitfalls are, and what their vision is. The competitive advantage they hope to have is normally captured in their vision. However, it doesn't always translate the same when it comes to real business.
- **Financial performance indicators**: We have spent quite a bit of time on this earlier in the chapter. Refer back to that section if you need to.

Importance of Management Quality

The quality of management in a company has a big impact on the success they achieve. Bad management is easy to disguise for a short while, but it will always become clear as time goes on. In addition to paying close attention to the financial statements, you should evaluate the quality of the people running the company.

A company that puts time and effort into appointing management that can drive the vision forward and invests resources to improve their management skills has a better chance to rise to the top in every aspect. You want to invest in companies that focus on having the right management team. A high stock price does not necessarily mean the company has good management. You need to look deeper than just the stock price.

The 4 Cs framework outlines essential characteristics of good management:

- **Candidness**: Owning up when something goes wrong is important. Reviewing past financial statements and commitments made by the management team and comparing them with what actually transpired is a great way to confirm whether the management team is trustworthy and capable of keeping their promises or admitting when they cannot.
- **Capability**: A company and its management team should be capable. This can be measured by taking a closer look at the individuals in the management team, the company's future vision and strategy to get there, how they manage their debt, and how resources are allocated.
- **Commitment**: A management team that is committed will ensure there is long-term value for shareholders. This can manifest in a number of ways including whether they personally own some of the shares and the compensation across the board (especially if the company is in distress).
- **Compassion**: This can easily be seen in how employees are treated and whether the management

team cares about them. Employee wellness should be a top priority for any company, regardless of what industry they are in.

Research and Evaluate Management Quality

These four characteristics are essential, but they may be difficult to spot without proper research and analysis. Let's look at a few ways that one can research and evaluate the management quality of a company.

Company Ratios

We've discussed most of the important ratios to look for in the first section of this chapter.

Management Team

As mentioned in the 4 Cs, it's important to look at each person individually in the management team, especially upper management. You can do a quick Google search, look at their LinkedIn profile, and scan for any articles that may mention them. This will help you understand whether they live and breathe the company values, even when they're not at work.

Some factors that you may want to look for include:

- Who were the founders of the company, and are they still part of the management team? If not, are they still linked to the company in any way?
- What are the qualifications of the people in upper management?
- What have they achieved during their career? Are there any noteworthy achievements, especially at the company they are currently working for?

- How long have they been with the company?

Depending on the company, the management team may be quite extensive. I would suggest that you at least look at the people in the following positions:

- Chairman and Vice-Chairman of the Board
- President
- Chief Executive Officer (CEO) and Deputy CEO
- Chief Operating Officer (COO)
- Chief Financial Officer (CFO)
- Chief Information Officer (CIO)

Management Compensation

When looking at management compensation, you need to take salaries, stock options, shares, bonuses, and any other benefits into account during a financial year or any other specified period.

It may be difficult to decide what compensation is considered "too high" for management, but you can use the Security and Exchange Commission website to review the U.S. executive compensation data and compare others' salaries with the company you are researching. Remember to compare like for like, i.e., if you're looking at the CEO's salary, compare it with a CEO's salary working in the same industry as the company.

If a company is doing well and its employees are also taken care of, there is no reason why the management team shouldn't be compensated fairly. However, it's a problem when the company is struggling financially, with poor ratios and unhappy employees, while management continues to earn high salaries.

Management Communication

Communication is key. The management team should be communicating with investors on a regular basis regarding any potential issues that the company may be facing that could influence the shares. In some cases, investors are only told once the issue starts affecting the business (or the bottom line), and by then, it's too late to make any decisions as an investor.

Although not required by law, a good management team would send shareholder letters to investors to alert them of any issues or provide a general update on the company. These letters are normally included in the company's 10-K annual report. If the company you are researching has shareholder letters, try to read some from the past few years to learn a bit more about the business and how the management team chooses to communicate. In some instances, you may find that they mentioned an issue that the company was facing at the time. Try to review the next few years' financial statements and 10-K reports to see whether this issue was addressed or not.

Chapter Summary

When assessing a business for investment, three primary considerations are crucial:

- **The financial health of the company**:
  - Knowing what the financial health of the company looks like is essential before buying any stocks.

Review the financial statements and analyze the various ratios.

- Look through the balance sheet and income statement and identify any potential red or green flags using the ratios and tips provided earlier in the chapter.

- **The competitive advantage**:
  - A company with a competitive advantage will always be ahead of its competitors and will be a golden opportunity for investments.
  - There are a few different competitive advantages a company can have:
    - **Cost leadership**: Maintains quality but can offer services and products at a lower cost.
    - **Customer service**: Focuses on customer service and makes sure that the customer is satisfied every step of the way.
    - **Differentiation**: Offers products and/or services of a higher quality or with more features.
    - **Focus**: Has a very specific target market that they cater to.
    - **Geographic**: Being strategically located close to suppliers, customers, or resources.
    - **Innovation**: Always ahead of the curve when it comes to innovation. They introduce new products and/or services to the market first.
    - **Speed**: Able to produce goods or deliver services quicker than competitors.
  - You can identify a company's competitive advantage by looking through customer reviews,

doing a market analysis, and looking at their financial performance indicators.

- **Management quality:**
  - ○ Management quality is a factor that is often overlooked but should be a fundamental check for investors. A company with poor management may not be a good investment choice. Bad management leads to bad decision-making, which may affect the bottom line of the company and have a knock-on effect on the company's shares and dividends.
  - ○ You can evaluate a company's management quality by looking at the following:
    - ▪ Financial ratios
    - ▪ Investigating the individuals of the upper management team
    - ▪ Looking at management compensation compared to other companies in the same industry
    - ▪ Reviewing past shareholder letters and comparing them to the subsequent 10-K annual reports.

You need to first understand how to evaluate a company for investment before you can decide on an investment strategy.

The next chapter deals with the different investment strategies, including long-term investing, short-term investing, value investing, growth investing, and dividend investing. We will compare the different strategies to help you choose the one that aligns with your financial goals and risk tolerance.

3

INVESTMENT STRATEGIES

Deciding which investment strategy to use can be quite a process. Everyone has their opinion and wants you to follow their method of investing. I'm here to tell you that there is no single perfect investment strategy. Every person's investment strategy should be different from the next and should be adapted as they grow older.

If your friend or an acquaintance has a set investment strategy and invites you over for coffee to sell it to you, you should be very cautious. I'm not saying you shouldn't go for coffee and hear them out, but don't buy their investment strategy. Here's why: Your investment strategy would most likely look vastly different from what they have put together. This is why I never understand how people "sell" their investment strategy or why others buy it. This is why knowledge is power. If you know that an investment strategy is something that should be individualized, you wouldn't take the bait and pay money for something that might not work for you. Other people may have had a lot of success with it, but that doesn't mean that you will, too.

An investment strategy should be based on your financial goals and risk tolerance. This doesn't mean that you can't take inspiration from others. Success stories are there for you to learn from them and use what works while adapting it to fit your needs.

We can learn a lot from Benjamin Graham (Kagan, 2024), known as the father of value investing. He was very disciplined with his investment strategy, which turned into immense success. He's been an inspiration to many, including Warren Buffett. His strategy mostly involved buying undervalued stocks and keeping those stocks long-term. Being undervalued doesn't mean that they are worthless. These stocks were so valuable, but nobody else saw their potential at the time, which is why Benjamin could capitalize on them. The only way he knew to do this was through thorough analysis.

Value investing is only one of the many strategies that you can consider. Let's take a closer look at the different investment strategies and how you can choose the best one for you. There is no foolproof strategy and they all come with their risks.

Long-Term Investing *Versus* Short-Term Trading

These are probably the most well-known two strategies. Most of the other strategies have some connection to either being long- or short-term, but they are also standalone strategies. You don't need to have a double-barrel investment strategy.

Long-Term Investing

Long-term investing means that you invest and forget. Okay, maybe not completely forget, but you get the point. You want to be in it for the long term. Most of the time, this means to hold on to investments for a year or longer. You need to have patience and discipline to use this strategy if you want to reap the benefits later.

Without patience and discipline, you may cash out on the investment too early because it's not doing as well as you want it to in a short period of time, or the investment may take a dip, and you get anxious. This is why I referred to it as "invest and forget." If you look at your investment almost daily, you might lose heart when it looks like things take a little dip. Keeping your eye on the long term will help you navigate this.

You can benefit more from an investment the longer you hold on to it because of the power of compound interest. People who still have a lot of time to grow their portfolio should make long-term investing part of their strategy.

Long-term investing has a few benefits, including but not limited to:

- **Lower transaction costs**: Every time you complete a transaction, there can be a fee connected to it. When you decide to invest long-term, you reduce your transaction fees, which means your gains are more. Instead of paying multiple transaction fees over a few years, you pay one transaction fee and see your money grow.
- **Reduced tax rates**: Long-term capital gains (investments held over a year) are taxed at a maximum rate of 20 percent, typically lower than

short-term gains. This only applies to brokerage accounts and not trades made through Roth IRAs and traditional IRAs.

- **The power of compound interest**: We have already discussed compound interest in detail in Chapter 1, but long-term investing is the perfect strategy to take advantage of it.

Some examples of long-term investments include growth stocks, real estate, bond funds, dividend stocks and value stocks, stock funds, small-cap stocks, and target-date funds.

Short-term Trading

Unlike long-term investments, with short-term trading, you want to hold on to an investment (specifically stocks) for a short period while it's profitable. This involves buying and selling stocks as the market fluctuates. Ideally, you want to buy a stock when the price is low but about to increase and sell it just before it reaches its peak to drop again. You can hold on to the stock for a matter of minutes or a few days. There is no set period that would qualify as short-term trading as long as you are capitalizing on the market fluctuations. Something to be careful of here is overtrading, but we'll cover this in Chapter 8.

This strategy is a lot more risky than long-term investing because it's volatile, and you need to buy and sell at just the right time. Although the risk is high, the reward can be just as good.

On the pros side, short-term trading can give you quick access to additional cash, you don't need a lot to start, and it has great liquidity. On the cons side, it does take a bit of time to get used to and learn the tricks of the trade, and it's difficult to make a profit when the market is very volatile, and the risk is quite high.

To decide whether you lean more towards short-term trading or long-term investing, here are some questions to consider:

- What are your financial or investing goals?
  Something that requires a lot of money, like buying a house, would fall more into the long-term investing category, whereas paying off immediate debt or going on a vacation could be more short-term. For example:
  - *I'm focused on building wealth for retirement, which* aligns with long-term investing.
  - *I'm saving for a down payment on a house within the next five years, which* may be a mix between the two or some medium-term investments.
  - *I want quick access to cash for short-term needs* that align more with short-term trading.
- Do you have a lot of free time to spend watching the markets and changing your investments when needed? If not, short-term trading is not a possibility. It requires a lot of dedicated time to ensure you don't lose money. For example:
  - *I have around 1-2 hours per week that I can dedicate to investing* would push you more towards long-term investing where you don't need to monitor it all the time.
  - *I enjoy analyzing stocks daily, and I have a flexible schedule* that can allow you to commit to short-term trading.
  - *I only have time to review my portfolio every few*

months, which is more aligned with long-term investing (with possible support from a broker).

- How much risk are you willing to take? Short-term trading comes at a higher risk (with the potential for higher returns), while long-term investing takes longer to mature but comes at a lower risk because time in the market is longer. With long-term investing, market fluctuations are not as relevant. For example:
  - *I'm comfortable with some fluctuations if I know there may be higher returns in the future* supports long-term investing.
  - *I am uncomfortable with high-risk investments and prefer stability* aligns better with long-term strategies.
  - *If it means that I can get quick gains, I'm happy to take some risks* leans toward short-term trading.
- Do you have patience when it comes to your investments to see the returns materialize? How patient you are or how quickly you lose heart will help determine your investment strategy. For example:
  - *I have quite a bit of patience and I'm willing to put in the time to see the return* fits into a long-term strategy.
  - *I need to see the returns materialize within a few months to a year* would be more aligned to short-term trading.
  - *I want to see immediate returns* is part of short-term trading with a high-risk approach.
- How soon do you need to access the money? The longer time you have to save, the longer your investment will be. For example:

- *I don't really need the money for the next 10 to 20 years* suggests a long-term investment approach.
- *I need it within the next 3 years* is more applicable to short-term trading or medium-term investments.
- *I may need the money in the next few months* is completely aligned to short-term trading.

- Do you have a lot of knowledge when it comes to financial metrics and do you understand how to perform market analysis?
  - *I know how to perform basic analysis but prefer simplified and hands-off approaches* leans toward long-term investment as well as index investing.
  - *I know how to analyze charts, understand financial ratios, and like to research stocks in detail* can suggest both long-term investing and short-term trading.
  - *I prefer an easy-to-manage strategy because I'm just starting out* would fit better with long-term investing with a very diverse portfolio.

- How often would you like to trade? Have you made provision for the transaction costs?
  - *I would prefer to avoid frequent transactions and minimize the fees* is for long-term strategies.
  - *I don't mind frequent transactions and the fees associated with it, as long as I get to capitalize on short-term market movements* is the definition of short-term trading.

Value Investing

This was Benjamin Graham's most common strategy (Kagan, 2024). Value investing is about finding and purchasing stocks the market has underestimated. Note that the key word here is *underestimated.* You really need to find the stocks that are *undervalued,* i.e., priced below what they are actually worth. Buying stocks only because they are *cheaper* and not because they are *overlooked* by other investors does not count as value investing.

I'm sure you can already see where the problem lies. There is always a risk that a valid reason exists for the low stock price. To buy the right stocks, you need to do a complete research and analysis to make an informed decision.

What you want to focus on is the intrinsic value and margin of safety of the stock. Intrinsic value is what something is actually worth. The intrinsic value will help determine whether the stock is worth more than what it's selling for and whether it is worth the investment.

The margin of safety is a percentage value of the difference between the company's fair value per share and what the current stock price is. A high margin of safety indicates that the stock is worth buying. Before you start researching stocks, decide what margin of safety you are willing to work with, and don't settle for anything less.

Conducting proper research, being patient, and remaining disciplined are the three keys to success for value investing.

A lot of value investors turn to a stock screener to help identify undervalued stocks. We won't get into that in detail in this book, but you can always read more about it on trustworthy sites like Investopedia or The Motley Fool.

Criteria you want to look at include:

- According to common guidelines, the price-to-earnings (P/E) ratio is preferably below 20, but the "right" P/E ratio ultimately depends on industry norms and the broader market context,
- The expected earnings per share (EPS) growth outlook for the next five years,
- Minimum return on equity (this is based on the industry but should be high),
- The minimum dividend yield and
- The PEG ratio is the P/E divided by the EPS growth. Ideally, this value should be less than one.

We discussed these ratios and how to determine them (or where to find them) in Chapter 2. Feel free to go back if you need a refresher.

Once you have a few stocks that meet the criteria, you need to start looking at the intrinsic value of each stock and compare it to the current price of the stock. Using the intrinsic value, calculate the margin of safety and identify those that meet your minimum margin of safety criteria.

It might feel like a lot of work, but if you don't do due diligence, you might lose quite a bit of money by buying stocks that are not worth it.

If you think you might like value investing, consider the following questions:

- Are you willing and able to put in the work to find the right investments? Finding a good value stock takes a lot of research and patience. Not everything that looks like a value stock is one.

- Can you wait for the investment to reach its full potential? With value investing, it could take quite a while for the investment's value to become significant.
- Will you be able to handle temporary underperformance without giving up hope? The stock is already undervalued and overlooked by others, so it will take some time to start performing the way you want it to.

Growth Investing

This involves buying stocks where the value is expected to grow at an above-average rate compared to other stocks. While many growth stocks are small or young companies, established companies like Amazon or Tesla are also considered growth stocks due to their continuous above-average growth potential. The stocks are often priced above their intrinsic value as the market anticipates significant future growth. Growth investors seek out these stocks early, aiming to derive significant value from them in the future.

This may sound a lot like value investing, but the big difference between the two is the fact that with growth investing, these are emerging companies that have the potential to become a big deal. With value investing, these stocks have been overlooked by other investors. They are not necessarily emerging companies, and there is no expectation that their value will grow at an above-average rate anytime soon.

You can find great growth stocks by following these simple steps:

- Analyze the market and identify powerful long-term market trends, like digital advertising, AI, cloud computing, e-commerce, etc. Focus on one or two; otherwise, your search may be too wide. You can always repeat the process for other trends.
- Identify companies that are in the best position to profit from the trend/s you chose.
- Take a closer look at the companies and identify their competitive advantages. We discussed the importance of competitive advantages, but they are especially important when you're considering using the growth investment strategy. You need to ensure that the emerging company or companies have a good enough competitive advantage that their competitors won't outshine them down the road.
- If your options are still too broad, prioritize companies that serve large markets. The bigger the company is, the more opportunity there is for growth.
- If you end with no companies, it just means that there may not be any good companies in that specific industry that have growth investment potential. Start the search using a different trend.

This approach can lead to higher long-term returns if the right stocks are chosen. The earnings from these stocks are usually reinvested, helping the company grow and allowing investors to benefit from compounding, which can significantly boost wealth over time. However, there are some drawbacks. These stocks don't pay dividends, so investors won't get regular income. They're also riskier because the market can be volatile, and competitors might outperform the company.

Here are some questions to consider if you want to go the growth investing route:

- Are you able to watch the industry trends closely and stay up to date? This greatly influences stocks, and especially growth stocks.
- Will you have the patience and discipline to stick to your guns, regardless of what the market says? With growth investments, there are fluctuations, and if a small dip is going to be too much, growth investing might not be for you.
- Are you okay with not receiving regular payouts? With growth investing, usually, no dividends are paid.

Dividend Investing

The last strategy we will look at is dividend investing, which means focusing on stocks where you are regularly paid dividends as a shareholder. You can choose what you want to do with the dividends. You can either save the money, spend it, buy more stocks by automatically reinvesting it into the same company, or diversify your portfolio and buy new stocks of other companies.

This strategy is ideal for investors looking for regular income from their investments. Stocks that offer dividends are typically associated with high-quality companies where earnings are predictable. In a company where the earnings aren't predictable, it will be very difficult to promise shareholders dividends.

Depending on the size of the dividends, you may have an increased tax burden from these dividends. Another quite obvious (but often overlooked) con is the fact that by paying dividends to shareholders, the company is not reinvesting that money into the company to grow faster.

If you want to get into dividend investing, here are some characteristics of a good dividend stock:

- **Qualitative**: Looking at qualitative features of a company includes the basics such as what they do, how long they have been in business, what industry they are in, whether the industry is doing well, what are the new innovations in the industry, and is the company leaning into that, etc. What you are looking for is financial stability—a company that is well-established and consistent with its results.
- **Quantitative**: You need to obviously analyze the company's financial data as well. Here are some quantitative features to look at.
  - **Dividend yield**: This is the first thing you need to look at and will probably help eliminate quite a few companies. Dividend yield can be defined as the value of return based on the stock you own. To calculate it, divide the dividend amount per share by the stock price, then multiply by 100 to express it as a percentage.
    - For example, if the stock price is $150 and you receive a dividend of $10 a year per share, the dividend yield is ($10 / $150) x 100 = 6.67%
    - It might be tempting to just rule out all the low dividend-paying stocks. However, a high dividend yield is not always a good thing. Instead of being drawn to high yields alone,

take the time to evaluate the company's overall health and growth potential using qualitative measures.

- In some cases, the dividend yield looks very high, but when you look deeper, you will uncover other issues. The high dividend yield sometimes causes investors to overlook bigger issues in the company.

- There's no single right answer for what constitutes a good yield. However, you may find these ranges helpful to begin with:
  - For large-cap and stable companies, anywhere between 2% and 6% is expected.
  - Stocks paying more than 6% may signal some potential risks. So, analyze them carefully.
  - For growth companies, the yield typically goes below 2%, which is expected given their more aggressive reinvestments.

- **Dividend growth rate**: Although it's important for a company to be stable, there should be a dividend growth rate over the years. You can access any company's past dividend payouts on their investor relations website (if they have one), some financial websites like Nasdaq, brokerage platforms like Fidelity, or data aggregators like Seeking Alpha.

Certain stocks hold the "Dividend Aristocrats" label. These companies have increased their dividends for over 25 years. You can find the full list online for the updated information.

This list can be a good starting point to look for dividend stocks.

- **Payout ratio**: The payout ratio of a company shows what percentage of its profit is given out as dividends. It's calculated as follows:
  - Payout ratio = Dividends paid / Net income
  - Although a high payout rate is great, you need to balance it with the need to reinvest profits into the company to improve it. In general, a lower ratio is more sustainable, but the dividend yield is lower.
  - Similar to dividend yield, there may not be an exact range; however, we can expect the following:
    - For mature and stable companies, 40%-60% is typical.
    - For companies who reinvest heavily for the growth, we can see it drop below 50%
    - If the ratio is higher than 60%, it can signal some risks unless the company is in the low growth stage and has a high cash flow. For example, utility companies may have such characteristics.
  - **Debt-to-profit**: We discussed a few financial metrics related to debt in Chapter 2, but debt-to-profit was not one of them. Ideally, a company should not have too much debt; that is a given regardless of the financial metric you're looking at. If they have too much debt, they may need to pay off the debt instead of sticking to their dividend payouts, which, although not the end of the world,

it affects your strategy. The whole point of investing in a dividend stock is to get dividends.

- The debt-to-profit ratio is calculated by dividing the total debt by the annual net profit.
- The lower this ratio is, the better. Keep in mind that there are some instances where getting into debt is not a bad thing, as long as the company can still meet all its obligations.
  - **P/E ratio**: We discussed this in detail in Chapter 2. Refer back to that section for more information.

Here are some examples (Table 3.1) of the dividend stocks from Bezek (2024):

Company (Stock)	Current dividend yield
Pfizer Inc. (PFE)	5.7%
Canadian Natural Resources Ltd. (CNQ)	7%
Hormel Foods Corp. (HRL)	3.6%
Washington Trust Bancorp Inc. (WASH)	6.7%
Magna International Inc. (MGA)	4.6%
British American Tobacco PLC (BTI)	8.3%

Table 3.1 Some examples of dividend paying stocks at the time of writing.

Chapter Summary

Choosing the right investment strategy from the beginning is important. However, don't be afraid to change your strategy when your circumstances change. This is why you should have a brief overview of the various strategies and not focus on only one. This book does not go into detail for each strategy (there is so much more you can learn!), so make sure that you choose one and do additional research.

Below, I have included a table summarizing the pros and cons of each strategy (Table 3.2).

Now that you have a good idea of the investment strategy that you may want to follow, we can start diving into investment accounts and how to navigate tax implications. You'll get a better understanding of the different types of investment accounts, the tax benefits associated with retirement accounts, and how to manage them effectively, including buying and selling stocks and understanding capital gains taxes. This way, you can make informed decisions to maximize your investment returns and tax savings.

Investment Strategies

Investment strategy	Pros	Cons
Long-term Investing	You don't need to worry about market fluctuations There are lower tax implications You take advantage of compound interest	You need patience (it takes a long time to get the desired results)
Short-term trading	You can make quick money There is great liquidity You can take advantage of market volatility instead of fearing it	Comes at a high risk You may experience high transaction fees It tends to be a full-time commitment
Value Investing	There is a possibility for significant returns	Thorough research is needed to ensure success
Growth Investing	You can expect high returns	There is generally high volatility Can be more expensive
Dividend Investing	You get regular income There might be some tax advantages Typically stable companies offer dividends, so your investment seems safer	Dividend cuts are possible The appreciation is slower than other investing strategies

Table 3.2 The pros and cons of different investment strategies.

4

INVESTMENT ACCOUNTS AND TAX IMPLICATIONS

Using a Roth IRA, Peter Thiel turned $2,000 into $5,000,000,000 (Malito, 2021).

Yes, it's a true story! And although Peter's story might not apply to everyone, there is no reason why you won't be able to derive value from investing.

Here is the disclaimer for the above story. It took quite a few years: In 1999, Peter's Roth IRA was worth less than $2,000. Twenty years later, in 2019, he reached $5 billion. He stopped contributing toward it in 1999, and it grew exponentially for the next 20 years. He did this by buying PayPal shares in 1999. When he started making gains, he invested the gains (still within the Roth IRA) to make new investments. Although he didn't physically contribute anything, the gains he got from these investments were used to grow his portfolio. This is a typical example of growth investing.

When it comes to investments, there are a few different types of investment accounts you can choose from.

Types of Investment Accounts

We will look at three main accounts, namely brokerage accounts, traditional individual retirement accounts (IRA), and Roth IRAs.

A brokerage account is set up through a brokerage, and it allows you to buy and sell different investments, like stocks, bonds, ETFs, etc. You can buy or sell investments and withdraw money anytime. You need to claim any capital gains in this account as taxable income, either short-term or long-term. There are different types of brokerage accounts as well, but we won't go into detail in this book. Some accounts include full-service brokerage accounts, discount brokerage accounts, robo-advisor accounts, brokerage accounts with a regional financial advisor, and online brokerage accounts, to name a few. There is no limit to how much you can buy and/or sell in this account.

With a traditional IRA, contributions are typically made with pre-tax income. Those who are ineligible for tax deductions due to income limits can contribute post-tax income. If you want to make any withdrawals in the traditional IRA, you will pay ordinary tax on those withdrawals. Once you turn 73, you have to start taking contributions out of the traditional IRA. There are no income restrictions or limitations when opening a traditional IRA (this is different for a Roth IRA, which we'll cover next). You have access to different investment choices, such as stocks, ETFs, CDs, bonds, etc. There is a maximum contribution per year that you can contribute towards a traditional IRA, which changes every year.

If you choose a Roth IRA, you contribute after-tax money toward the account, which means all your earnings grow tax-free, and no tax deduction will apply if you withdraw from it after age 59½. This only applies if the account has been open for at least five years. The types of investments available are the same as a traditional IRA. There are some exclusions for Roth IRAs, such as collectibles, S-corp stock, and coins. A Roth IRA is the preferable investment account if you think you might move into a higher tax bracket in the future. To be eligible for a Roth IRA, you need to meet certain criteria. This changes annually and is based on your Modified Adjusted Gross Income. If you don't qualify for a Roth IRA, you can always opt for a traditional IRA.

Let's compare the three in terms of the key features, benefits, and limitations (Table 4.1).

Type of investment account	Brokerage account	Traditional IRA	Roth IRA
Key features	A variety of investment options Great liquidity Taxes paid on gains	Annual contribution limits You pay tax upon withdrawal	Same annual contribution limits as traditional IRA Contributions toward the account are after-tax money
Benefits	There are no limitations for buying or selling You can access your money at any time with no penalty No age limits	Your investments can grow tax-deferred until withdrawal Focuses on Retirement Tax deductions on contributions	Growth is tax-free Can withdraw contributions tax-free at any time
Limitations	Overall capital gains can be reduced due to tax	Penalties for early withdrawal Have to start withdrawing contributions by age 73	There are income limits Have to keep earnings for at least five years before withdrawing tax-free

Table 4.1 A Comparison of three investment and retirement accounts.

Tax Benefits of Retirement Accounts

We've briefly mentioned the tax benefits, but let's take a closer look at how opening an IRA account can help reduce your taxable income and enhance your overall retirement savings.

Tax-Deferred Accounts

The two common types of tax-deferred accounts are traditional IRAs and 401(k) plans.

When opening a traditional IRA, you can get tax-deferred growth within the account on all earnings and contributions. Taxes are only applied when you begin withdrawing funds, and these withdrawals will be taxed at your ordinary income tax rate.

As mentioned before, there is a limit to how much you can contribute to the traditional IRA annually, and this tends to change with inflation.

The most obvious (and immediate) advantage is that paying money into a traditional IRA before tax reduces your taxable income, and you pay less tax now. Another benefit is that by the time you retire, you may be in a lower taxable income bracket, which means that the tax rate will be lower.

Tax-Exempt Accounts

Roth IRAs are the most common tax-exempt accounts.

By choosing a tax-exempt account (like a Roth IRA), you get future tax benefits instead of a tax break with contributions. If you choose to withdraw your earnings during retirement, these withdrawals are tax-free, provided that the account has been open for at least five years.

Just like a traditional IRA, there is a limit to which you can contribute annually. There is also an income limit, which means that not everyone qualifies to open a Roth IRA.

Although these accounts are not used regularly, they are perfect for younger individuals. People shy away from them because they only get the tax benefit years later. But on the positive side, you can access any contributions you made into

the account tax and penalty-free, and the earnings can be accessed tax-free after retirement.

Whether you choose a tax-exempt or tax-deferred account, both of these will help to boost your retirement savings. The sooner you start your account and invest, the more earnings you will accumulate.

The following two scenarios can further explain the differences between these accounts:

Scenario 1: Traditional IRA

Lisa wants to save for retirement. She is in a high tax bracket (32%) now and anticipates to be in a lower tax bracket after retiring.

How Lisa Benefits:

- Lisa contributes $6,500 to a Traditional IRA (the annual limit for 2024).
- She qualifies for a full tax deduction because her income is below the limit, reducing her taxable income by $6,500 this year.
  - Tax Savings: At a 32% tax rate, Lisa saves $2,080 in taxes this year.
- Her investments grow tax-deferred, meaning she won't pay taxes on the gains until withdrawal.
- At age 65, Lisa retires and begins withdrawing from the Traditional IRA. Her retirement income places her in the 12% tax bracket.
- She only pays 12% taxes on withdrawals, which is much lower than her current 32% rate.

Lisa was able to reduce her taxable income today and defer taxes to retirement when her tax rate is lower.

Scenario 2: Roth IRA

DAVID WANTS to start saving for retirement early. He is in a low tax bracket (12%) today and expects to earn significantly more in the future.

How David Benefits:

- David contributes $6,500 to a Roth IRA (the annual limit for 2024) using after-tax money. He pays $780 in taxes upfront (12% of $6,500)
- His contributions don't provide an immediate tax deduction, but his investments grow tax-free.
- At age 45, David decides to withdraw $30,000 to help with a down payment on his first home.
- He can withdraw his contributions tax and penalty-free.
- At age 60, David begins taking withdrawals in retirement. Both contributions and earnings are completely tax-free because he met the holding period and age requirements.

David pays taxes now while in a low tax bracket and enjoys tax-free growth and withdrawals when his income is higher in the future.

Buy and Sell Stocks

Before you can get into investing, you need to open an account. Here is a step-by-step guide on how to open each of these.

Brokerage Account

- **Step 1: Decide what type of brokerage account to open**. There are a few different types of brokerage accounts to consider. You need to decide which one you need before opening it. The type will depend on your investment objectives. You can decide between cash and margin. There are also retirement brokerage accounts, but we'll deal with IRAs in the next section.
  - Traditional cash brokerage account: This type of account requires you to put money into the account to buy stocks.
  - Traditional margin brokerage account: With a margin account, you can borrow money to buy stocks in addition to the money you deposited.
- **Step 2: Find the brokerage with the best fees**. Compare different brokerages to find the best deal. Some brokerages offer discounts or no fees at all for certain transactions, like a discount when transferring large amounts or no transaction fee for buying and selling stocks. Some may also charge a commission fee, while others waive this commission fee if certain criteria are met.
- **Step 3: Consider the benefits**. Although the fees are important, you also need to look at any other benefits the broker offers you with the account.

- o **Research**: A good brokerage will provide access to research and appropriate financial information that will help you with your investments. This can include access to research from third-party firms and stock ratings.
- o **Convenience**: Although we've moved into a digital world, sometimes meeting someone face-to-face or on the phone to discuss issues and ask questions is a lot more convenient than trying to navigate it digitally. If this is something that you like, try to find a broker that offers this service.
- o **Fractional shares**: For new investors, this might be especially important. Most new investors don't have the money to buy full shares of large companies, and a brokerage that offers fractional shares is one of the benefits that attract young investors.
- o **Foreign trading**: You may have access to trade on international stock exchanges if your account allows you to convert money into a foreign currency.
- o **More features**: There are many other features they may offer, so make sure that you compare what each brokerage offers and check that it meets your needs.
- **Step 4: Choose a brokerage**. Consider the pros and cons based on steps 1, 2, and 3 above to determine which broker is better for you.
- **Step 5: Open the account**. For most brokers, you can open an account by completing an account application form online. They ask a few personal information questions like your driver's license and

Social Security number. Only individuals 18 and older can open their own account.

- **Step 6: Put money in the account**. There are a few ways you can put the initial money into the account. Some accounts may have a minimum amount that needs to be transferred initially. You can transfer money via a wire transfer, electronic funds transfer, asset transfer (if you're transferring it from another investment), or checks.
- **Step 7: Check investments and stocks**. You've already done some research on stocks and investments you want to focus on. Now, you can start putting it into action.

Traditional IRA

- **Step 1: Choose a type of broker**. For a traditional IRA, you still need to find a broker. Ideally, if you want to open a traditional IRA, you should choose between an online broker or a robo-advisor. If you want to be hands-on and manage most of the transactions yourself, an online broker would be best. If you need some help or want your investments to be automated, you can choose a robo-advisor. If you don't want to use a broker, you can choose to use a bank as well. Most banks offer traditional IRAs.
- **Step 2: Find a broker or bank**. Whether you want an online or robo-advisor or use the bank, there are a few options you can choose from. Explore different options to find one with low fees that offer the services you need.

From here, the steps are the same as opening a broker account. You want to open an account online, add money, and start investing.

Roth IRA

- **Step 1: Check your eligibility**. Before you open a Roth IRA, make sure that you meet the requirements. There is an income limit as well. If you earn over a certain amount (this changes annually), you can't open a Roth IRA. There aren't any age requirements; however, you need to have earned an income to contribute. The sooner you start, the more you will benefit from compound interest.
- **Step 2: Gather your documents**. You need some documentation to open a Roth IRA. You will need:
  - A copy of your government-issued ID (like your driver's license or passport).
  - Details of the beneficiaries you want to add to the account.
  - Personal details, like your Social Security number. You will need to confirm other information like your phone number, full name and surname, address, etc.
  - Your banking information.
- **Step 3: Choose a financial institution**. You can choose from a few financial institutions to open your Roth IRA. Do some research in terms of the fees and services offered, any minimum account requirements, customer service, and the investment strategies offered.

- **Banks**: In some instances, the bank might require you to have a checking or savings account with them before you can open a Roth IRA. By having both at the same institution, you may be able to contribute to the Roth IRA a lot easier.
  - **Online brokerage or robo-advisor**: We've briefly touched on these when discussing the brokerage account.
- **Step 4: Opening the account**. How you open the account will depend on the financial institution you choose. It could be either an online application or in-person.

After this, the steps are the same in terms of putting money into the account and selecting investments for your Roth IRA. You should manage your Roth IRA on an ongoing basis. Monitor the progress and make changes as needed, but don't check it daily. The idea is not to make investment changes too often but when it's required.

Buying and Selling Stock in Your Roth IRA

There are a few assets you can invest in within the Roth IRA, like mutual funds, annuities, stocks, bonds, real estate investment trusts, and ETFs. If you choose a self-directed Roth IRA, you can also invest in cryptocurrency, private replacement securities, precious metals and other commodities, and promissory notes.

The following restrictions apply. You can't invest in anything related to life insurance or collectibles, like coins, artwork, stamps, alcoholic beverages, and gems.

Something that is great about a Roth IRA is the fact that the earnings are all tax-free, so you don't have to worry about capital gains. You can trade as often as you want. If it's your first time and you don't have a lot of experience, I would suggest that you take advice from an expert on when to trade.

Because you can grow your investments tax-free, there are some restrictions when it comes to trading within a Roth IRA. One such restriction is that you can't use anything in the Roth IRA as security to get a loan. There is no margin account option.

When it comes to investing, you need to spend some time considering the asset allocation of your funds. You can split between stocks and other investments, keeping in mind that the majority of your earnings will be in stocks. Investing in other assets is just a safety net so that all your eggs are not in one basket.

The best way to determine this ratio is to calculate your risk tolerance—the amount of risk you can take. As a general rule of thumb, your stock allocation should be approximately 100 minus your age. For example, if you're 20, then 80% of your funds in the Roth IRA should be for stocks. The other 20% can be made up of various other assets.

Stocks are riskier, which is why the percentage of stocks should decrease as you get older.

Keeping Track

Regardless of the investment account choice you make, it's important to keep track of every transaction made within the account. Make sure that you save copies in multiple formats in case you need them later.

For some accounts, this may be needed for tax purposes when you need to file taxes on capital gains. Even if you have a Roth IRA, keeping a record of the transactions can be useful. By keeping track, you can ensure that you stick to the annual limits (if applicable), how much you have contributed (for Roth IRA, so you know how much you can withdraw tax-free before retirement), and in case there are any questions later on.

Capital Gains Taxes

Capital gains specifically refer to the profit realized when you sell an asset for more than you purchased it. Unrealized increases in value are not considered capital gains. The difference between the current value of an asset and what you originally paid for it is known as the capital gain. Capital gains are only realized when you sell the asset. This means that you will only need to pay taxes on an investment's capital gains at the point of sale and not while it is appreciating.

There are two different types of capital gains: short- and long-term gains. Short-term gains are connected to short-term trading (i.e., on assets you've had for a year or less), while long-term gains are connected to long-term investing (i.e., on assets you've had for more than a year).

Whether it's long- or short-term gains, you need to submit and claim these on your annual tax return. They are taxed differently, and understanding the difference is important when determining your investment strategy and calculating your trades.

The tax rate on short-term gains matches your ordinary income tax rate. Long-term capital gains, though, usually have lower tax rates than ordinary income. However, the rate you pay depends on your income and filing status, like whether you're single or married. For the most updated rates, you can refer to the IRS website.

Minimize Taxes

There are a few ways to minimize the taxes on investments. Here are some strategies you can apply to manage and minimize taxes while still benefiting from your investments.

- **Choose tax-deferred retirement plans**: By choosing a tax-deferred investment account (like a traditional IRA), you only pay taxes once you start taking contributions from it. This could work to your advantage because you don't pay tax on every transaction. Chances are, you may be in a lower tax bracket by the time you need to start withdrawing from the fund, meaning that you pay even less tax.
- **Invest long-term**: By investing long-term, you pay a lower tax rate on capital gains. Because you hold onto these assets and don't trade them frequently, you'll only pay capital gains taxes once upon sale.
- **Offset gains and losses**: If you have experienced some losses, you can sell the investment around the same time as the gain, and the two will offset each other to a degree, meaning you pay less tax. I know we don't like thinking about losses, but they do happen. You may as well take advantage of it.
  - For example, if you have two investments, one has gained 20% while the other suffered a loss of 12%. If you sell both, the net gain will be less, resulting in less tax payable.

- **Holding periods**: If the investment is on the cusp between a short-term trade and a long-term investment (i.e., just less than one year), consider the option of holding on to the investment for a little while longer so that it's classified as a long-term investment to reduce the tax payable. This is provided that the investment has been quite stable, and the additional months, weeks, or days won't depreciate your investment value.

Chapter Summary

- Choosing the type of investment account you want is the next step in your investment journey. Understanding your investment needs and goals will help you to choose the right account for you.
  - **Brokerage account**: With this account, you can deposit money at any point, trade, and access your money whenever you want with no penalties. This is funded with after-tax money, and you pay taxes on capital gains.
  - **Traditional IRA**: This account has no income restrictions. However, there is a limit to how much you can contribute to it annually. You can use either pre- or post-tax money, and any withdrawals (even at retirement) are subject to tax. This is a tax-deferred account, which means you don't pay taxes on capital gains or interest earned.
  - **Roth IRA**: Not everyone qualifies for this type of investment account. There is an annual

contribution and income limit. This account is tax-exempt, meaning that you don't pay any tax (even on withdrawals). You can withdraw contributions at any time. However, earnings can only be withdrawn after age 59½, provided that your account has been open for at least five years. If you withdraw earnings before this age, you will incur penalties.

- To manage your investments effectively, it's important that you understand the tax implications and how to manage capital gains tax. There are ways to minimize this by choosing a tax-deferred or exempt account, investing long-term, offsetting gains and losses, and analyzing your holding periods.

Successful investing relies heavily on risk management to protect and increase returns in the long run. In the next chapter, you will learn essential strategies to manage investment risk, such as the importance of diversification, setting realistic investment goals, and understanding individual risk tolerance. These tools should help protect and support your long-term financial growth.

RISK MANAGEMENT

I n 2008, the world experienced a financial crisis (Singh, 2024). The housing market collapsed, causing a ripple effect in the financial sector and economy. A few factors played a role here, and many people were affected, some more than others.

Many people suffered great losses during this financial crisis, even with their investment portfolios. What became clear during the crisis was that those with diversified portfolios were in a better position than those who invested everything in the financial sector. Although the financial sector is an excellent place to invest, the fact that they didn't have investments elsewhere means that their entire portfolio suffered a loss. In cases of diversified portfolios, losses were partially mitigated by sectors that weathered the crisis well.

Before the 2008 financial crisis, it was common for many investors to favor the financial sector. There was no real reason or known threat since everyone perceived the financial sector to be a safe bet with high returns. Once the housing market started diminishing, it was too late, and most investors were hit hard.

By diversifying your portfolio, you won't be immune to sector crashes, but you can limit the effect it has on your investments. This chapter is all about understanding risk and diversification.

Risk and Return

This is a constant theme in investments. Where there is a return, there will always be risk. Most of the time, the risk is directly proportional to the return. The higher the risk is, the higher the reward may be; however, the reward is not always guaranteed.

This is where the risk-return tradeoff comes in. When investors consider a risky investment, they trade the risk off with the potential return. If the risk is worth the return, they take the plunge. This is not just a feeling they get or a gamble—it's based on tangible factors, such as their risk tolerance, whether they will be able to recover the loss, and how much time is left before they retire. Another factor is the time you plan on remaining invested.

The risk may be lower if you plan on investing for the long term. However, with the same asset, the risk could be much higher if you only want to remain invested for a short time. This is because if you invest for longer, there is more time to recover, and you're able to ride out the market lows and offset them with market highs. Where the investment period is short, the market fluctuations increase the risk significantly.

The risk-return tradeoff also depends on whether you apply it to that single investment or take the entire portfolio into account (provided that the portfolio is diversified). If a diversified portfolio is at play, the risk is a lot lower.

Whenever you make an investment decision, you should always consider the risk-return tradeoff. There are three main ways you can calculate the risk-return tradeoff called the alpha ratio, beta ratio, and Sharpe ratio.

Alpha Ratio

The alpha ratio determines any returns in excess of the benchmark index. It is a calculation of whether an investment earns more or less than the benchmark return.

- If α is positive, it means that the asset outperformed the benchmark index.
- If α is zero, it means that the asset didn't under or overperform the benchmark index.
- If α is negative, it means that it underperformed compared to the benchmark index. This doesn't necessarily mean that it's a bad investment, but just that it didn't perform favorably. You may need to do further analysis.

Beta Ratio

This calculation shows you how much the investment price moves when compared with the overall market or benchmark index. Usually, the Standard & Poor's 500 (S&P 500) index is used.

Although there are formulas to calculate the variance and the co-variance, these are normally readily available on financial sites and even brokerage sites.

- If ß is equal to one, this means that the price of the investment or stock moves at the same pace as the market. So, if the market goes up by 5%, so would the stock.
- If ß is greater than one, it means that the stock is more volatile than the market, i.e., when the market goes up by 5%, the stock might go up by 15%.
- If ß is less than one, it means that the stock has less volatility than the market. If the market goes up by 5%, the stock might only go up by 2%.
- Sometimes, ß may be negative. This means that the stock moves in the opposite direction than the market, i.e. if the market goes down, the stock goes up.

Sharpe Ratio

This ratio helps to determine how well a stock is performing compared to the risk it poses. Investors can determine how much excess return they earn for each unit of risk they take.

- If the ratio is one or above, it means the investment is earning more per unit of risk. The higher the number, the better.
- If the ratio is above zero but below one, it means that it is earning a positive return per unit of risk, but it may not be worth the risk.
- A negative ratio indicates that the stock is failing to perform and presents an undesirable risk.

When assessing the risk-return relationship, it is crucial to consider all three ratios collectively. Relying on just one may create a misleading impression of the stock's actual performance and result in an inaccurate evaluation of risk.

Let's explore an example together:

Imagine we want to invest in the stocks of SAMPLE company, and we found the following ratios after our research.

- Sharpe Ratio: 1.2
- Beta (β\beta): 1.3
- Alpha (α\alpha): 2.5%

Step 1: We first analyze the Sharp Ratio

- For every unit of risk, the stock yields 1.2 units of return, as indicated by its Sharpe Ratio of 1.2.
- This is a strong Sharpe Ratio, suggesting the stock offers good returns relative to its risk.

Step 2: Let's look into the Beta Ratio

- The beta of 1.3 indicates that the stock is 30% more volatile than the market. In other words, SAMPLE's movements are expected to be 30% greater than market fluctuations.
- While the stock provides favorable risk-adjusted returns as measured by the Sharpe ratio, its higher beta implies increased sensitivity to overall market trends and, therefore, greater systematic risk.

Step 3: Finally, we explore the Alpha Ratio

- An alpha of 2.5% indicates the stock provides an additional 2.5% return beyond what its beta predicts.
- This shows that SAMPLE's performance is not solely due to market movements. The stock's performance, or its management's actions, surpasses market predictions, presenting a potentially powerful investment for those aiming for active gains.

Based on these ratios, we can conclude that SAMPLE is a high-risk, high-reward stock with great risk-adjusted returns (Sharpe Ratio of 1.2) and excess performance (alpha of 2.5%). The stock's beta of 1.3 indicates higher volatility; therefore, it's more appropriate for investors comfortable with greater risk.

Why Diversification Matters

We've spoken a lot about diversification up to this point. In essence, it's ensuring that your investment portfolio consists of various assets and touches different industries or sectors. As we saw from the 2008 financial crisis, it's not only important to have different types of assets but also to invest in different sectors in case an entire sector is impacted.

You might not start your portfolio diverse because we all need to start somewhere. But as you add more investments to your portfolio, keep in mind that you want to diversify it.

The key is not to diversify just for the sake of it. Many people misunderstand this concept and approach it the wrong way, blindly buying different stocks without conducting a thorough analysis of each one.

Think about it—why would you invest your money in a business you don't truly believe in when you already have another stock you trust more? For example, if you hold only one stock in your portfolio and can't find other high-quality options, don't feel pressured to add more just to achieve diversification. Quality should always come before quantity.

A diversified portfolio generally consists of three main components:

- **Cash investments**: Money markets and CDs form part of short-term cash investments. Money markets may produce a lower return rate than bonds and stocks because the risk is lower.
- **Bonds**: Bonds usually fluctuate less than stocks and provide steady interest payments; however, overall economic factors, like interest rate shifts, can still affect them. They tend to be more stable and a good addition to any investment portfolio.
- **Stocks**: The majority of your investment portfolio will consist of stocks, especially if you're still young. This can be domestic or international stocks or a combination thereof.

It doesn't mean that your portfolio should have all of these. Every person's investment portfolio would look different, but this is a good framework. You can also choose to include other assets, such as real estate, sector funds, and asset allocation funds.

Benefits of Diversification

Diversification helps you minimize your investment risk. There is no way to predict the future, so nobody really knows which investments are solid and which ones are better to stay away from. We have explored quite a few tools to help you analyze companies and choose the most promising ones, but it's never a sure deal. To mitigate the possibility of loss, you need to diversify your portfolio.

Just because your portfolio is diverse doesn't mean that you will have higher returns than someone with a less diverse portfolio. If you aim to maximize your returns in a short time, diversification is not going to help you get there. Someone with a less diverse portfolio may seem like they are earning more in the short term, but over a few years, a diverse portfolio can outperform the other because of normal fluctuations. If one asset or industry drops, there are many other assets (and industries) that can offset the loss.

It might sound counterproductive, but the key is to have assets that grow in opposite directions. Stocks and bonds tend to have this relationship, which is why most investors own a collection of stocks and bonds.

Here are two additional ways in which you can diversify your portfolio:

- **Different industries**: When you invest in stocks, you should also diversify the industries in case something happens for the one to collapse or go through a dip. This is why it's good to invest in existing indexes, like the S&P 500.
- **Big and small companies**: Don't focus on only big and well-known companies. You might find a

diamond in the rough and discover the newest value investment.

The Swensen Model is often used to demonstrate a well-diversified portfolio. It consists of:

- 15% treasury inflation-protected securities,
- 15% government bonds,
- 20% real estate funds,
- 5% emerging-market equities,
- 15% developed-world international equities, and
- 30% domestic equities.

This is very diversified and might be what your portfolio looks like after a few years. Another example is Ramit Sethi's Diversified Portfolio, which consists of 83% stocks, 15% bonds, and 2% cash (short-term investments).

Setting Realistic Investment Goals

The best goal-setting methodology I've come across is the SMART goals. You can use this for any type of goal, even financial and investment goals.

The first step to setting goals, before we get to SMART goal setting, is to define your goals. You need to decide where you're planning to build wealth. Are you saving for a holiday? Planning for retirement? Investing for a down payment on a house? Want to open your own business? Define your financial goals at a high level.

Next, you want to take those financial goals and add a bit of detail to them by creating SMART goals. You may have more than one SMART goal for each of the overarching financial goals; that's completely normal. The more you can define it and break it into smaller goals, the easier it will be to achieve.

A SMART goal is a goal that is specific, measurable, achievable, realistic, and time-based. If a goal meets the criteria of a SMART goal, you have a bigger chance of reaching it. One missing element may result in the goal not being fleshed out enough, and it may make it more difficult to achieve (or you may not know when you have achieved it).

Here is a detailed breakdown of exactly what a SMART goal is.

- **Specific**: The goal has to be specific and with no grey areas, stating exactly what needs to be done.
- **Measurable**: There needs to be a way to measure your progress and know when you have achieved the goal.
- **Achievable**: It needs to be something under your control that you can manage and achieve. For example, your goal, saying that the stock market should go up by 50%, is not something that is in your control.
- **Realistic**: It needs to make sense in your current circumstances. For example, setting a goal to be a millionaire in a week when you currently have $50 is not realistic.
- **Time-based**: You need a timeline to track your progress and have a cut-off for when you want to achieve it. Without a timeline, there is no motivation to help you chase the goal.

By having these SMART goals, you have clear guidelines

outlining exactly what you are chasing, which makes your investment decisions a lot easier.

Let's look at an example.

I want to save to go to the Maldives for a holiday.

That alone is not a very SMART goal. It might be specific because it mentions Maldives and that you want to go on holiday; however, you don't know how much you need to save, so there is no way to measure your progress. Whether it's achievable or realistic is unknown because there isn't enough information. There is also no timeframe in which the goal should be completed.

Let's take that same goal and make it SMART.

I want to save to go to Maldives for a 2-week holiday in December 2027. I need to save $15,000 for flights and accommodation.

Using the SMART methodology, let's analyze it:

- Specific: Is the goal specific? Yes, I want to go to Maldives for a holiday and spend two weeks there.
- Measurable: Is it measurable? Yes, I know that I need to save $15,000 in total for this holiday.
- Achievable: Is it achievable? That would depend on the income and investment strategy. At the time of writing, that goal is three years away. That gives me 36 months to save. If I am able to generate at least $417 a month for the next 36 months, I will have enough money.
- Realistic: Is it realistic? Definitely, if saving this amount per month fits within the budget or investment plan.

- Time-bound: Do I have a timeline that I need to stick to? Yes! I know that I need to save the money by December 2027.

The third step is to decide what your investment objective is. There are four main investment objectives (strategies):

- **Growth**: Most of the time, this is the initial goal. Most people who get into investing do it to grow their money for various reasons. Choosing growth means that you are in it for the long term and want to see your wealth increase over the years by taking risks.
- **Cash flow**: This is simply to bring in a constant flow of money (like income) through your investments.
- **Preservation**: Most people who are in or near retirement invest for preservation reasons. They simply want to preserve the funds they have and not see it run out. They don't take a lot of risks and stay on the safe side because there is no desire to grow their money at this point.
- **Lifestyle maintenance or improvement**: This includes paying off debts now so that you have more disposable income in the future or spending money on improving your lifestyle now. What this looks like is up to you.

Now, all you need to do is track your SMART goals and ensure that you're working towards them. Try to arrange them according to when they need to be achieved (based on the time aspect) and focus on the ones that you want to achieve first. Once you've arranged them, make sure that they all still make sense. For example, if you have $50,000 debt that you want to pay off in the next three years and you also want to go on a trip to Paris in the next year, which will cost you around $20,000, you may need to reprioritize your goals and decide what you want to focus on the first one.

Risk Tolerance

Your risk tolerance reflects how comfortable you are with the possibility of investment losses. This is not something that you can calculate using mathematical equations, and it will be different for each person. This is an important factor to consider when investing so that you don't lose sleep every night because of the potential losses you are experiencing. Managing risk in alignment with your personal risk tolerance can effectively regulate your stress levels.

Risk tolerance can be grouped into three primary categories:

- **Aggressive risk tolerance**: Choosing an aggressive approach means that you are open to high risk in exchange for potentially high returns. An aggressive approach includes assets like venture capital and cryptocurrencies. Those with an aggressive approach accept that they may lose everything. This might be a good approach if you are still young and have time to recover from setbacks.
- **Conservative risk tolerance**: A conservative approach means that you're more careful than others and don't particularly want to take on much risk. This may mean that the returns are on the lower side and growth is slow, but it's the price to pay for conservative investing. An example would be a certificate of deposit

(CD). The investment grows at a set rate and is kept for a predetermined amount of time. There is a guarantee of return, although very low. Most conservative investors are on the older side since they don't have time to recover if they suffer any losses.

- **Moderate risk tolerance**: This is a balance between aggressive and conservative. Most of the time, a moderate risk tolerance portfolio consists of 60/40 stocks *versus* bonds. The 60/40 split is a common starting point, but allocations can vary based on individual circumstances. Some moderate investors might adopt a 70/30 or 50/50 split, depending on their goals.

Determining Your Risk Tolerance

Although you can't mathematically calculate your risk tolerance, a few factors will influence it, which you can measure. Sometimes, we feel that we are willing to take the risk; however, this may not always align with our financial ability to do so. Things that you may need to take into account include:

- How important the financial goal is: Here, the importance is not measured on a personal level, i.e., how important you feel it is. But rather how important it is to your financial well-being. If the investment is helping you to become debt-free, that is quite important, and you may consider a moderate approach *versus* saving for a holiday (which is not essential to your financial well-being), in which case you would take a more aggressive approach.

- Your needs: As the financial urgency increases, the willingness to take risks diminishes. Approaching the moment of financial need prompts individuals to adopt a more conservative approach, prioritizing the preservation of funds over potential gains to avoid losses right before the crucial time.
- The time you have: The more time you have to grow your money, the higher your risk tolerance may be. For example, if you're saving for retirement and you're still young, your risk tolerance may be a lot more aggressive. As you approach retirement, your risk tolerance will become more moderate, and you will eventually switch to conservative to keep the money you have already accumulated.

Here are some questions that you can ask yourself when determining your risk tolerance:

- *What investment objectives do I want to focus on? Do I want to grow my investment, maintain my lifestyle, or save for retirement?*
- *How does this tie in with my financial goals?*
- *Do I have time to accumulate funds, or do I need them urgently?*
- *Can I afford to lose everything I invest?*

Your willingness to take risks is one thing; the financial ability to do it is something entirely different. You need to find a balance between the two. If you're not willing to take much risk but you have the financial ability to do it, you may not meet your financial goals. The opposite can also be true: If you are willing to take risks but you don't have the financial ability to do it, you may lose it all.

Considering both is crucial when investing to ensure that you make the best of the opportunities you have.

Chapter Summary

- The risk of an investment is often directly proportional to its potential return. Riskier investments may offer higher returns, but they also come with a greater chance of significant losses.
- The risk-return tradeoff can be analyzed and considered using three metrics: the alpha ratio, beta ratio, and Sharpe ratio. Each measure is different, and they should all be calculated and considered in an investment decision.
- Creating a diverse portfolio is essential to minimize the effect of market fluctuations and industry changes.
- You can create a diverse portfolio by including different types of investments. You can also include assets from different industries and invest in both large and smaller companies.
- To reach your investment goals, it's important to set SMART goals.
- How much risk you can accept is determined by your risk tolerance and your financial resilience to losses.
- There are three types of risk tolerance: aggressive, conservative, and moderate.
- Your risk tolerance is impacted by how important the

financial goal is, your cash flow needs, and the time you have.

- To make the best investment decisions, you need to find a balance between your appetite and financial ability for risk.

Managing your risk is essential; however, you also need to know how to deal with market volatility. In Chapter 6, you will learn how to manage your investments during market volatility by staying calm, maintaining a long-term perspective, and implementing risk mitigation strategies.

6

DEALING WITH MARKET VOLATILITY

I n the early 2000s, many investors faced significant losses when tech stocks plummeted during the dot-com bubble burst (Delossantos, 2023). Some investors cut their losses and sold everything, while others remained calm during the storm. They maintained a long-term perspective and continued to invest in solid companies. These investors saw their portfolios recover from the crisis and grow in the years following.

A bubble is created when the stocks of a certain industry suddenly increase more than those of other industries, creating a bubble of rapid growth. Due to market volatility, there is no certainty of when the bubble will burst. For example, no one saw the dot-com bubble burst before it happened. Once they did, it was already too late to prevent losses. The best thing they could have done at that moment was to ride the wave and see whether things improved.

Herd mentality is very common when there is an investment bubble. Many individuals have various conjectures about potential future events. Don't blindly follow what others say, and focus on your own goals. Make sure that you apply the concept of portfolio diversification to try to minimize any potential losses.

Staying Calm During Market Downturns

Although market volatility is not something you can control, your behavior in response to it is something you can. How an investor behaves during a rise or fall in the market can greatly influence their portfolio. Some investors might change their investment approach completely, while others stick to their guns.

Our emotions and cognitive biases profoundly influence our investment choices and financial decisions, particularly during times of market instability.

The editorial team at Howard Capital Management (2024) notes that fluctuations in the stock market significantly influence investor behavior, prompting numerous studies on the subject. While the efficient market hypothesis (EMH) asserts that all pertinent information is incorporated into market prices, leading to rational decisions, this premise frequently fails during turbulent times when emotions and uncertainty dominate the landscape.

Another theory that is used especially during high volatility is the prospect theory. This theory is based on the understanding that we fear possible loss more than we value possible gain.

How this translates in the investment market is that investors are more likely to keep stocks that are currently losing value hoping that they will rebound and sell those that are performing well in fear of them crashing.

Market volatility can elicit feelings of fear and anxiety, causing investors to make impulsive decisions. According to research (Engelberg & Parsons, 2016), there is a clear link between a decline in the stock market and mental health hospital admissions.

Although it's never an exact science, based on the studies already performed, we can characterize investor behavior by these patterns during high market volatility:

- **Flight to safety**: When there is uncertainty, some investors change their investments to safer options, moving from an aggressive or moderate approach to a more conservative one, where their money is safe.
- **Overreaction and underreaction**: This is when investors either overreact to news, i.e., there is a small dip in the market, and they decide to sell everything (even unaffected assets), *versus* underreaction, where an investor isn't moved by the news that should change their investment choices.
- **Disposition effect**: This is in line with the prospect theory, where investors are quick to get rid of assets that are appreciating but hold on to assets that are depreciating in the hopes that they will change.
- **Selective perception**: This occurs when investors are selective about the information they choose to accept. They tend to gravitate towards information that is

aligned with what they already believe about their investments and ignore anything that might contradict their opinion.

- **Herding behavior**: Following the herd is when investors listen to what everyone else has to say and follow their advice instead of relying on their own research and financial goals.

There are a few ways you can navigate the volatile market without making any impulsive decisions you may regret later. The above behavioral patterns are all grounded in biases. It's important that you know what your bias is so that you're able to recognize it when you start relying on it. By recognizing your bias, you're better equipped to take a step back and go with a more rational approach.

In addition to this, a diverse portfolio will always help. We've discussed this in detail in Chapter 5. Having a diverse portfolio can safeguard you against market volatility and help you sleep better at night.

Here are some additional tips to help you:

- Keep your goals in mind: You've set your SMART goals. Focus on them when you're making your investment decisions. When you focus on them, you won't get distracted when there is a small fluctuation in the market.
- Focus on the long-term horizon: If you keep checking on your investments daily, small changes in the balance may cause a bit of anxiety. Focus on the long-term horizon and try not to check the investments too

often. As long as you remain updated on investment news and can identify any changes, it's best to let your investments grow in peace.

- Investing is usually better than cash savings: For short-term needs or emergency funds, cash savings are preferable. However, for long-term growth, investments tend to outperform savings accounts.
- Let history comfort you: We have gotten through some pretty rough global recessions and market crashes. The good thing? The market and investments always recover. Although we can't predict the future, remember this the next time it feels like everything is crashing.

Strategies to Mitigate Risk During Volatile Times

There are a few strategies that you can follow to reduce risk during periods of market volatility. We'll look at three in this chapter.

Diversify

Diversifying your portfolio spreads risk among different asset classes. We've covered this in detail in Chapter 5, so feel free to refer back if you need to.

Dollar-Cost Averaging

Whether you're new to investing or a seasoned investor, it's still difficult to time the market just right. Sometimes you get lucky, and sometimes you don't. Timing the market can be very exhausting, and we rarely get it right.

Dollar-cost averaging is a great way to disregard market volatility without feeling overly anxious about your investments. It involves investing the same amount of money in the same asset at regular intervals, regardless of the current price. So, instead of investing $10,000 upfront, you may choose to invest $100 on the first of every month for 100 months.

By doing this, there is no pressure to determine exactly when the price would be perfect. You get 100 opportunities to invest, and one of them is bound to be lower than the others. The way this works is your $100 may buy you five shares this month and six shares next month because the price of the share (or index) changes with the market fluctuations.

Dollar-cost averaging can be applied to many investments, including index and mutual funds, through most brokerage accounts or traditional IRAs. Most 401(k) plans through an employer work this way. As the employee, you choose the amount and the investment, and your employer regularly purchases securities based on your investment choice. The number of securities added monthly may differ more often than not because of dollar-cost averaging.

Let's look at an example of dollar-cost averaging (Table 6.1). The amount contributed per month is the same; however, because the price per share varies, the number of shares bought also varies. This is an example and does not reflect a real asset or index.

Month	Amount contributed	Price per share	Number of shares bought	Total shares
1	$50	$5.50	9.09	9.09
2	$50	$5.70	8.77	17.86
3	$50	$5.30	9.43	27.29
4	$50	$4.50	11.11	38.4
5	$50	$4.10	12.2	50.6
6	$50	$4.10	12.2	62.8
7	$50	$4.45	11.24	74.04
8	$50	$4.95	10.10	84.14
9	$50	$5.10	9.8	93.94
10	$50	$4.70	10.64	104.58
11	$50	$4.75	10.53	115.11
12	$50	$5.05	9.9	125.01

Table 6.1 An example of dollar-cost averaging.

After 12 months, the person above owns 125.01 shares. If they used their $600 and bought shares upfront for a price of $5.50 per share, they would have only received 109.09 shares. That's a big difference and definitely changes the potential return as well. This may not always be the case, and it all depends on the market condition and the volatility of the stock.

This is a strategy often used by new investors because it helps you get into the habit of investing, and you don't need to know too much about the market or investing to get started.

Benefits

The benefits might seem obvious, but they're important to highlight.

- You experience less anxiety around market fluctuations.
- You get into the habit of regular investing, which makes it easier to build wealth over time.
- You often spend less on average due to fluctuating prices, especially if the market experiences dips. If you bought the same number of assets upfront at a high price, you might end up paying more overall.
- You avoid the common mistake of investing when the prices are on the rise. Although you do purchase during those times, you also purchase at times when it's low.
- Helps reduce emotional decision-making during market fluctuations by automating your investments.

There is only one time when dollar-cost averaging has a disadvantage, and that's when the price keeps rising. In that case, it would have been better to buy once-off.

There are five simple steps to get you started with dollar-cost averaging:

1. Decide what investment you want to go with. This can either be an individual stock or mutual or index funds. Although we have gone through the process of choosing the right stocks, you can also opt to go for an existing fund that is already diversified on the stock market.

2. Next, speak to your broker or use an online platform to set up an automatic investment plan for your chosen asset.

3. Figure out how much you can afford to invest regularly. The aim is to invest for years, not weeks or months. When determining the amount, you need to make sure that you can sustain the investment for the entire duration. The longer you can invest, the better.

4. Now that everything is in order, set up an automatic plan. This ensures that your payment is made at your chosen intervals, and you never forget to invest. Your broker will be able to help with this automatic process, where the shares are automatically purchased with the invested funds without you needing to manually intervene.

Dollar-cost averaging is an effective way to take advantage of a volatile stock market without being overwhelmed by its fluctuations.

Cash Reserve

It's important to have some cash reserves or an emergency fund on hand when you need it so that you don't have to sell any assets if you find yourself in a financial pickle.

Cash reserves should make up a small but sufficient percentage of your overall financial plan, enough to cover emergencies without hindering long-term investment growth. The reason why you shouldn't put too much of your portfolio toward cash investments is because of the opportunity you lose to increase your gains. Cash investments like certificates of deposit (CDs) are typically safe but offer lower returns compared to riskier assets like stocks or some bonds.

In saying that, cash investments are still important. The exact percentage you need is based on your personal situation, but they are great for emergencies.

An emergency fund is money set aside for when emergencies happen. You can decide what constitutes an emergency, but in general, it will be things like losing your job, a sudden illness, a car accident, a natural disaster, or something similar. Of course, if you have insurance, most of these will be covered, but you can still use your emergency fund for any shortfalls. The amount in your emergency savings should cover at least three to six months of your regular expenses.

If any of these happen and you don't have an emergency fund, you may have to resort to selling some of your assets, which is not ideal.

Historical Market Trends and Lessons

By looking at some of the historical market trends, we can learn valuable lessons and pick up a few tips on how to manage the market.

There have been a few crashes in the market that have affected investments, like the crash of 1929, Black Monday in 1987, and the COVID-19 pandemic in 2020. These are only three major events; there were a few more.

In the aftermath of the 1987 crash, investors who stayed invested saw positive 1-year, 3-year, and 5-year returns.

However, recovery from the 1929 crash was much longer, taking over two decades to return to pre-crash levels, regardless of how badly the market was hit at the time.

Looking at History, here are five lessons we can learn:

1. Historically, markets have always recovered from downturns, though the timeline for recovery can vary significantly depending on economic and global conditions.
2. This isn't the first time that we are experiencing volatility, and it won't be the last. Being patient during these volatile times and remaining calm is key to getting through it.
3. If you focus on the long term and maintain a portfolio of quality assets, market volatility's impact is significantly reduced as markets tend to recover over time.
4. If you create a diverse portfolio, you will be in a better position and less affected by any market fluctuations.
5. Risk and volatility are inseparable aspects of investing. While higher risk can lead to higher rewards, not all risks result in gains, so careful analysis is essential.

Chapter Summary

- You can't control market volatility, but you can control your behavior amid fluctuations.
- How we respond in uncertain times is determined by our psychological biases and emotions.
- Investor behavior in uncertain markets can be explained by prospect theory, focusing on decisions

under uncertainty, and the efficient market hypothesis (EMH), which assumes markets reflect all known information.

- There are five main patterns seen in investors:
  - flight to safety, where they change their investments to safer options;
  - overreaction and underreaction, where they either overreact to news or do not react at all when they should;
  - disposition effect, where they sell assets that are doing well and keep assets that are losing value;
  - selective perception, where they only accept information that aligns with their bias and
  - herding behavior, where they follow what everyone else says.
- You can remain calm during market volatility by keeping your goals in mind, focusing on the long-term horizon, understanding that investments often outperform cash savings over time, and remembering that markets have historically recovered after downturns.
- There are known strategies to mitigate risk during market volatility, which include diversification, dollar-cost averaging, and cash reserves.
- Volatility is not new, and it will always be around. Managing it and setting up your portfolio to mitigate the effects is key.

A balanced portfolio is the crucial next step in managing risk and achieving long-term success. In the next chapter, you will learn how to create and maintain a balanced investment portfolio by employing effective asset allocation strategies, conducting regular portfolio reviews, and making necessary adjustments over time. This helps you meet your financial goals while managing risk and adapting to life changes.

BUILDING A BALANCED PORTFOLIO

Hopefully, by now, you have noted quite a few tips and strategies that will help you set up the best portfolio for you. A successful portfolio is balanced and reviewed regularly to ensure it still meets your financial needs and goals.

To put it another way, imagine your favorite music streaming app recommended songs that didn't match your taste; you'd skip them, right? The same is true for investments. Your portfolio needs to be carefully curated and adjusted to reflect your financial goals and risk tolerance.

In this chapter, we'll explore how to create a portfolio that feels personal and customized to your specific needs. From asset allocation to regular rebalancing, these strategies will help you stay on track and grow your investments effectively. Let's dive in!

Asset Allocation Strategies

Asset allocation means dividing your investment portfolio between various assets for diversification, such as fixed-income assets (like bonds), equities (like stocks), and cash or cash-like equivalents (like money markets). It's the cornerstone of a balanced portfolio. How you allocate assets is based on your risk tolerance, investment horizon, and financial goals.

A balanced portfolio can be defined as a collection of diverse investments (assets) that have been carefully designed to balance risk and return. Without proper asset allocation, it's impossible to have a balanced portfolio.

You don't have to reinvent the wheel when it comes to asset allocation. There are a few known strategies that you can apply.

- **Age-based asset allocation**: Using age-based allocation means that you subtract your current age from 100. This will determine what percentage of your portfolio should be allocated to stocks that are usually higher in risk and volatile. As you become older, this percentage will decrease. Some brokers may increase the initial number to 110 or 120, given the recently increased life expectancy.
- **Constant-weight asset allocation**: This involves regularly rebalancing the portfolio by buying more underperforming assets and selling portions of outperforming ones to maintain the initial allocation proportions.
- **Dynamic asset allocation**: This strategy is used quite often and involves making investment decisions based

on the highs and lows in the market and adjusting your portfolio accordingly.

- **Insured asset allocation**: This is a good strategy for investors who are very opposed to risk. They can set a base asset value (floor) on their portfolio, and as soon as the value drops to that amount, there are immediate steps, like reallocating to lower-risk investments, that mitigate the risk of their investment portfolio depreciating even more.

- **Life-cycle funds asset allocation**: An investor can choose from pre-determined funds known as life-cycle funds. These have been set up by professionals for every life stage of an investor based on the general age, risk tolerance, and possible investment goals. The portfolio is already set up, so there isn't much you need to do. Although this can be a good approach, many investors need individual solutions based on their personal goals and appetite for risk.

- **Tactical asset allocation**: With this strategy, there is an increase in portfolio adjustments to focus and capitalize on short-term investment opportunities, aiming for optimized risk-adjusted returns

Asset Allocation Examples

Let's take a look at three different asset allocation scenarios for individuals with low, moderate, and high-risk tolerance. For these examples, we'll use the age asset allocation for the initial setup. Remember, these are just examples and should only be used as inspiration to create your own.

Investor 1: Low-Risk Tolerance

This investor is already retired and wants to maintain his current lifestyle. He is 65 years old with a low-risk tolerance. He definitely can't afford to lose any money and needs to preserve what he has. His asset allocation could include:

- 30% stocks
- 45% bonds
- 25% cash

Although, based on age asset allocation, his stocks should be 35%, this can be slightly adjusted based on his current financial situation and ability to take risks.

Investor 2: Moderate-Risk Tolerance

This is a middle-aged investor, about 45. She plans to retire at 60, giving her 15 years until retirement and a moderate risk tolerance. She can't afford any major losses. Based on her age, her portfolio might look something like this:

- 55% stocks
- 40% bonds
- 15% cash

Investor 3: High-Risk Tolerance

This would be a younger individual, let's say a 25-year-old man. He is 40 years from retirement and has a high-risk tolerance. He wants to grow his retirement savings and is willing (and financially able) to take risks. Here is a potential asset allocation for his portfolio:

- 75% stocks

- 18% bonds
- 7% cash

He can take more risks with stocks or might opt for high-risk indexes.

Regular Portfolio Review

The above is a good start for these individual investors. However, in a year or two, they may need to make a few changes. Regularly reviewing your portfolio helps keep you on track to meet your investment goals and spot areas needing adjustments. A portfolio review should be performed at least once a year or whenever anything changes, such as your financial status or investment objectives.

Perhaps you already started an investment portfolio before you really knew what needs to be considered. This section will help you review your portfolio and make sure that it meets the guidelines and your individual needs.

When the time comes to review your portfolio, remember to include everything in the review. You need a complete overview of your financial situation. Make a list of all your assets, liabilities, income, and expenses.

Some questions you may want to consider before reviewing your portfolio, include:

- In what life stage are you? How many years are left before you want to retire? Based on your current situation, is your ideal retirement age feasible?

- Based on the above, what would be your ideal asset allocation?
- Has your investment objective or investment goals changed since the last time you reviewed your portfolio? If so, how?
- Do you still have the same risk tolerance and ability to take risks?

Considering these questions before the review will help you when you're stuck in the details of your portfolio and provide some direction on whether things are still on the right track.

Once you're ready to get started, here are a few guiding principles to help you with the review.

- **Assessing your asset allocation**: You need to make sure that the current asset allocation in your portfolio still meets your needs and is in line with your investment goals. Good diversification is important while still ensuring that your portfolio is set up to meet your goals. This is mostly applicable if you didn't initially consider asset allocation.
- **Analyzing equity investment categories**: This involves ensuring that the investments within your assets are also diversified within different sectors. You can discuss the top industries with your broker to ensure that you're tapping into the right sectors. Make sure that the ones you chose for your current portfolio still serve you and help to meet your needs.
- **Evaluating worldwide investment allocation**: Having a balance between well-established and emerging markets is a great way to find a potential

growth investment. If you initially chose an emerging market, evaluate its performance over the last year compared to other emerging markets and decide whether you want to keep or change it.

- **Evaluating bond funds**: The viability of bonds fluctuates with interest rates. It's important to evaluate the bonds you have invested in and adjust them if necessary.

- **Determining cash reserves**: An investment portfolio should include cash reserves. If you need to withdraw some cash from this part of your portfolio or your financial situation has changed demanding an increase in the reserves, this is the time to make the change. Devise a plan to top up your cash reserves or increase it to match your current lifestyle.

Whether you're in the process of reviewing your portfolio or not, staying updated on the markets is crucial for investment success. By staying updated on trends and opportunities, you can update your investments as things start shifting in the market. Be careful not to be too sensitive to market fluctuations and the next best thing. As discussed before, sometimes an investment is not worth the hype, and you end up losing your money. When something new emerges, or a new trend starts, do the necessary research and make an informed decision.

You can watch sites like Bloomberg, CNBC, Yahoo Finance, and Reuters for more information about different assets or emerging trends.

Rebalancing Your Portfolio

After reviewing and assessing your portfolio, rebalancing is the next step; however, you may decide to rebalance at other times, too.

To rebalance your portfolio means that you adjust the asset allocation back to your original target mix. The target mix was the initial percentages for your portfolio divided between stocks, bonds, and cash reserves, which may evolve over time based on changes in your financial goals or risk tolerance.

As your investments grow, stocks may outgrow bonds as well as cash reserves, and eventually, your investment portfolio might shift from 75/18/7 to 85/10/5 (stocks/bonds/cash investments). You can get it back to the target mix by rebalancing, selling some of the assets that are overperforming, and buying more of those that are underperforming to get back to the right percentages. For example, you would sell some stocks, buy more bonds, and allocate extra money into your cash investments.

Alternatively, you can always add more money into the portfolio and invest it into bonds and allocate some towards cash investments instead of selling any stocks. This will also restore the balance.

By rebalancing your portfolio, you manage the risk by maintaining your desired risk-return profile.

There are three main strategies when it comes to rebalancing your portfolio and the timing related to it.

The first strategy is calendar-based rebalancing. This approach requires rebalancing your portfolio at regular intervals (i.e., annually, biannually, quarterly, etc.). Once you decide on the interval, stick to it regardless of market fluctuations and movements.

The second is threshold-based rebalancing. Here, you decide on a specific percentage that an asset can deviate from the target percentage and take action as soon as it reaches the threshold. For example, if your stock percentage is 75%, you might set a threshold of 5%. Once it increases to 80% or decreases to 70%, you take action to restore the balance.

The third method is a combination of calendar-based and threshold-based rebalancing. This means that you have specific times at which you will rebalance, but you also establish thresholds. So, you still rebalance at the set time but are also sensitive to thresholds. If anything changes in the market and you need to make changes, you can do so immediately based on the threshold instead of waiting until it's time.

Before you rebalance your portfolio, take note of how much your portfolio has deviated from the target mix, whether your target mix is still applicable and appropriate in your current situation, and whether your goals or risk tolerance has changed.

To rebalance your portfolio, you can follow these easy steps:

- **Analyze**: This should be part of your portfolio review. This is where you analyze the current percentages of your asset allocation.
- **Compare**: Once you have the current percentages, you can determine how far they deviate from the ideal percentages you decided on. This is also where you need to make a call whether it has drifted too much

and needs a rebalance or whether you are comfortable with the percentages.

- **Sell**: You can choose to sell the outperforming asset; most of the time, it will be stocks due to the nature of how they grow in value over time. However, keep potential tax implications in mind.
- **Buy**: Using the additional funds from selling, you can buy more of the underperforming asset. It doesn't mean it's actually underperforming in terms of appreciating, but it simply means that it grows slower than the overperforming asset.
- **Add money**: Along with the rebalancing, you can also choose to add additional funds to your portfolio. You can use the same method to calculate the allocation towards every asset. For example, if you want to add $10,000 to your portfolio, $7,500 may go toward stocks, $1,800 toward bonds, and $700 toward cash investments.

Adjusting Your Strategies as You Age

Your financial goals and risk tolerance will evolve as you grow older. While you're still young and have quite a bit of disposable income, you can invest more and typically take on more risk. As your responsibility increases and your disposable income decreases, you may not have as much to invest. You'll also start taking a more conservative approach the closer you get to retirement age to ensure that you still have a proper nest egg to spend during retirement.

If you take on too much risk close to retirement, there is a possibility that you could lose a large portion of your investment, and you won't have as much time to build it up again. Because of this, you need to adjust your investment strategy and objective as you age.

Though individual risk tolerance varies, typically, when you look at younger investors, most of them are growth-orientated. They are willing to take risks so that they can grow their investment as much as possible. Their asset allocation and choice of investments reflect a growth strategy and sometimes aggressive approach.

Taking a closer look at older investors who are approaching retirement, they take a more conservative approach with little risk because they focus a lot more on capital preservation and income.

Your 20s: Getting Started

The sooner you begin, the better. By getting started in your early 20s, you give yourself enough time to take calculated risks, grow your investments early, and take full advantage of compound interest.

This is the perfect time to start with a diversified portfolio, focusing on growth-oriented stocks, index funds, or ETFs to maximize long-term growth. Investing regularly and being disciplined about saving are two great habits to start cultivating in your early 20s.

You should also set up your Roth or traditional IRA during your 20s. Although you might not have thousands to invest in your 20s, due to sustained growth over time, even a small monthly contribution will make a big difference. Not having a lot to invest in your 20s is not an excuse to wait until your 30s. You lose years of compound interest.

In your 20s, consistency is key.

Continuing in Your 30s

This is a lot like your 20s. You can still take calculated risks and be somewhat aggressive, aligned with your growing responsibilities because you have the time to recover if something goes wrong. By now, you likely have accumulated a solid foundation, which would have been harder to achieve if you delayed investing until your 30s.

Your portfolio should still be focused on growth and remain diversified in terms of asset allocation and industries. You might be able to add larger assets to your portfolio at this point, such as real estate, if your financial situation permits it.

You might start to get the hang of things now and be more comfortable with making your own decisions instead of relying on index funds, though index funds can still be a reliable option for steady growth. Remember to still consult with a financial advisor when you need to.

Although your focus might be on raising children and buying a house, don't neglect your retirement plan.

In your 30s, the aim is to grow your investment and reach stability within your portfolio. Review and rebalance based on your investment objective and plan.

Making Changes in Your 40s

If you didn't start adjusting your portfolio in your late 30s, your 40s is definitely the time to do it. Consider moving to a more moderate approach to align with your mid-life priorities.

Although you should constantly be checking your progress toward your financial goals, it's especially important in your 40s to ensure that you are tracking well toward retirement. Time for high-growth investments starts to diminish in your 40s, but you can still focus on growth, especially in the early part of the decade if retirement is further away. The mid to late 40s might prompt you to adjust your investments as your risk tolerance, financial goals, and life circumstances evolve.

At this point, include a mix of assets with long-term growth potential and more stable investments to balance growth and risk.

Preparing for Retirement in Your 50s

Depending on what age you plan to retire, in your 50s, you may consider moving from a moderate to a conservative approach.

Once you get to your 50s, you don't have a lot of time to grow your investment and almost no time to recover if something goes wrong, especially if retirement is near. The focus should be on generating income and preserving your investments with an emphasis on stability. You need to protect the savings you've built up to this point from market fluctuations and any potential crashes.

You need to review your portfolio and make strategic shifts to ensure your asset allocation is in line with your risk tolerance and investment goals at this stage of life. If possible, try to increase the contributions towards your IRA or 401(k) to boost the savings.

Your 60s and Beyond

Once you retire, your aim should be to generate a sustainable income through your investments while still protecting the balance as much as possible. You want to be able to enjoy life during retirement and not worry that you will run out of funds halfway through. None of us know our exact lifespan, but with increasing life expectancy, it's wise to plan for the possibility of living into the 90s or beyond.

Because of this, it's important to have a primarily conservative approach to protect funds, with a small allocation to growth-oriented investments to combat inflation and stretch the portfolio as far as possible. You can't afford significant losses to market fluctuations because there is no time to recover.

Devise a strategic withdrawal plan that will provide you with a steady and regular income while also keeping long-term growth prospects in mind. The money that remains in your investment can continue to appreciate over time.

Chapter Summary

- Creating a balanced portfolio is the key to a successful investment strategy.
- The cornerstone of a balanced portfolio is effective asset allocation. This means that you divide your portfolio between various assets to create diversification.
    - The percentage of allocation will depend on your risk tolerance, investment horizon, and financial goals.
    - The most well-known asset allocation strategies

  are age-based, constant-weight, dynamic, insured, life-cycle funds, and tactical.

- It's important to regularly review your portfolio to ensure that it still meets your needs and that you are getting the value you hoped for.
- Rebalancing your portfolio is usually done during periodic reviews or when an asset's performance significantly deviates from the target allocation.
- To rebalance your portfolio means that you restore the balance in your asset allocation to the target mix, or a new percentage if you need to make any adjustments.
  - You can choose calendar-based rebalancing, threshold-based rebalancing, or calendar- and threshold-based rebalancing.
  - To rebalance, you need to start with an analysis of the current portfolio and compare it to what it should be. You may sell any over-performing assets and buy more underperforming assets. You can also allocate more money to your investment based on the preferred percentage allocation.
- You need to regularly reassess your investment strategy to ensure that it ages with you and continues to meet your changing needs at every life stage.

Even if you have a well-balanced portfolio, you still need to know how to avoid common mistakes when it comes to stock trading if you're after long-term success. The last chapter deals with common mistakes in stock trading, such as emotional investing, overtrading, chasing hot stocks, and ignoring fundamental analysis. It aims to help you avoid these pitfalls and become a more disciplined and successful investor.

COMMON MISTAKES AND HOW TO AVOID THEM

R esearch suggests that emotions play a significant role in investment decisions, potentially influencing the majority of choices, particularly during periods of high market volatility (Khan, 2023). This supports the finding that mental health admissions increase whenever there are fluctuations in the market (Engelberg & Parsons, 2016).

A classic example where investors allowed their fear to make their financial decisions is the 2008 financial crisis. They sold their stocks at significant losses due to the immediate situation and fear of no recovery, despite historical evidence that the majority of assets tend to rebound over time. This period highlights the critical importance of avoiding emotional investing and focusing on the fundamentals.

Emotional Investing: Fear and Greed

Making all of your investment decisions based on your feelings is known as emotional investing. This can be dangerous because our emotions are fleeting. They change based on the weather, how someone else speaks to us, and how our morning coffee makes us feel. Basing a big financial decision on that can have detrimental results.

We are still human, though, and emotions are not bad. You should sense your feelings fully, but when making financial decisions, it's best to take the emotion out of it. Easier said than done, I know. It's a lot less effort to choose stocks that seem to be performing well and not worrying about diversifying or overtrading due to market fluctuations.

The truth is that a financial loss hits us harder than an equivalent gain. If we lose $10,000, it will have a bigger impact on us than gaining that same amount. Because we are more sensitive to loss, we tend to use our emotions to dictate how and when we invest.

The two most common emotions when it comes to investing are fear and greed. Most investors experience fear when the market takes a dip. During this time, they might sell their stocks for a loss, fearing that the stock market won't recover. When the market hits rock bottom, most investors are hesitant to buy because they don't know when the market will have an upturn.

As soon as it starts getting better, they might still be cautious until there is a clear sign that the market is on the rise again. At this time, they become optimistic and may even lean towards greed in the hopes that the market will reach a new high soon. This feeling of greed results in buying overpriced stocks.

There are three key heuristics that every investor should be aware of (and avoid):

- **Gambler's fallacy**: Although gambling and investing are not even in the same camp, it's easy to fall into a gambler mentality when it comes to investing. It's based on the idea that something is more or less likely to happen based on previous experience. For example, if you flip a coin four times and all four times it lands on heads, you might bet on the fact that it will land on tails the next time because it's bound to happen. Although that may or may not be the case, our brain tells us it should happen. This unsure probability creates a false sense of security.
- **Overconfidence bias**: This is our belief that we are better than we actually are. There is nothing wrong with having confidence and knowing your worth, but overconfidence bias can lead to a false feeling of safety. In investments, we may think that we are experts and that any gains are due to our skills. We believe that we always make the right decisions and underestimate the risk of certain trades. There are some other biases you should be aware of as well.
  - **Loss aversion bias**: making irrational decisions in the fear of losing. Always playing it safe and not taking on any risk.
  - **Herding bias**: This is the same as following the herd. You enjoy feeling included and participating in discussions. They lead, and you buy or sell.

- **Recency effect**: We pay less attention to long-term trends and more to recent occurrences. For example, when asked how things are going, we tend to focus on recent events and not what happened the entire year. This affects us mostly when we have a bad experience with investing. Instead of focusing on how the market has been performing, we focus on the recent crash and are hesitant to invest again.

While it seems easy to ignore emotions when investing, it's actually quite challenging. These actionable steps will assist you in avoiding emotional investment.

- **Define your goals and time horizon**: When you have clear goals and have a set time to remain invested, you're less likely to make emotional decisions. This is why it's important to have clear SMART goals and regularly monitor your progress toward them. Focusing on long-term investments will remove the need to constantly watch the market, and you will be less likely to be swayed by immediate fluctuations.
- **Bucketing approach**: This is the perfect method to use when you have different time horizons for your financial goals. Using SMART goals, you should create short-, medium-, and long-term goals. By using the bucketing approach, you can have three buckets of investments: one for each time horizon. This will also help not to affect your investments for your other goals when you need to make a change.
- **Investment strategies**: Focusing on your investment plan, keeping a diversified portfolio, and dollar-cost

averaging are all investment strategies that will help remove the emotion from investing.

- **Turn to the professionals**: Don't forget to speak to your financial advisor before you make big investment decisions. They have a lot of experience with the market and will be able to give you objective advice based on your current situation and financial goals. Because they're not in the midst of the problem, they can give a different perspective without involving emotion.

Overtrading and Its Pitfalls

Overtrading means excessively and constantly buying and selling assets. Although there is no law against this for individuals, brokers may face regulatory consequences because they may generate more commission without regard to a client's best interests. The following are potential causes of overtrading:

- **Boredom**: When investors have too much time on their hands, and they stare at a screen all day, they sometimes end up overtrading just to do something.
- **Greed**: Once investors get a taste of profits, they may start to perform more transactions to keep experiencing that high.
- **Over-excitement**: When there is a sudden surge of a stock and the potential to make a quick buck, investors may jump at the opportunity without proper research.
- **Vengeance**: After experiencing several losses or one

significant loss, it's common for investors to start overtrading to try to compensate for the loss.

One of the risks of overtrading is increased transaction fees, which directly impact your returns. Depending on your brokerage account, you may pay a transaction fee for every trade that is completed (This fee is more common in options trading, a topic beyond this book's scope). Let's say each transaction costs you one dollar. For the initial investment, you pay one dollar, and you keep the investment for a year. That means you only paid one dollar in transaction fees. If you decided to complete ten trades every month for that year, you would have paid $120 in transaction fees, which means you paid $119 more than if you just stuck to one transaction. You could have kept that $119 in the investment and made more profit from it.

Another area that is affected is taxes. We dealt with taxes in Chapter 4, so refer back to that chapter if needed. The more capital gains you have, the more tax you need to pay, even on quick, small trades.

The last one to be aware of is the potential for poor timing. By overtrading, you might catch the market at the wrong time. For example, let's say you buy a stock today for $10. Tomorrow, the price drops to $8, and you sell it. The next day, it increases to $12, and you buy a share again. A day later, it drops again to $11, and you sell it. Overall, there was a loss. If you bought it for $10, held onto it for a few days, and then sold it for $11, you would have made a profit. The timing in the market was off, and because of overtrading, there was a loss.

Avoid Overtrading

The first step to avoid overtrading is the awareness that it exists and that we're all susceptible to it. The urge to consistently trade in line with what's happening in the market is something that could be difficult to control, especially if there are no trading fees involved. Here are some practical steps to help you navigate overtrading.

- **Set some rules**: Setting some rules and keeping yourself accountable is a good way to avoid overtrading. You can make a rule that you're only allowed to trade once a month or only allowed to perform two transactions when trading. You can even set a rule that you're not allowed to invest unless you've reviewed the financial statements. Whatever will work for you, set those rules and stick to them, regardless of how good the deal looks. Ensure the rule aligns with your investment strategy and market conditions.
- **Don't give in to emotional investing**: We've covered emotional investing earlier in this chapter. Make sure you avoid it.
- **Take a break**: Sometimes, we get so stuck in what we're doing and so committed to doing it well that we lose focus of what's important. Taking a break from trading and leaving your investments for a while could help to avoid overtrading. By not constantly checking your investment, you won't feel the need to make changes all the time.
- **Know when to stop**: Just like with gambling, overtrading can become impulsive. You need to know when to step away from the computer. Once you catch

yourself falling into the trap of overtrading, take a step back before you lose too much.

- **Don't lose focus on your long-term goals**: We stop worrying about the current market fluctuations when we keep our eye on the future.

Chasing Hot Stocks

Chasing hot stocks might seem exciting and like a good idea. A hot stock could be any stock that other people keep raving about, one that may be doubled in value in a week, or any other sign that shows it's suddenly performing really well. If you're chasing hot stocks, it means that you keep looking for the "next big thing" based on other people's opinions or what the market is doing at the moment. The problem is by the time you want to get on the hype train, it's almost too late.

A popular stock is not always the best investment decision. People tend to make investment decisions based on market opinion or what their neighbors say. By jumping on the same train, you're running the risk of losing. Just because a stock is trending does not make it a smart investment decision. Before investing, remember to do due diligence.

There are some key lessons we can learn from chasing hot stocks.

- **Unrealistic expectations**: We often have unrealistic expectations when it comes to hot stocks. Even though we know that the market is volatile, we still expect the stock to continue to increase in value based on the recent history. The reality is that there will be fluctuations, and you need to time it just right if you want to benefit. This leads me to the next point.

- **Timing**: It's very difficult to get the timing right. By the time it becomes a trend, and you decide to invest, it might be too late. The stock may already be at its peak, resulting in a loss for you. Some investors with expertise in technical analysis may achieve success; however, it is not recommended for everyone.
- **Concentration risk**: When something looks like a really good deal, we tend to put all our money in that single deal. This opens us up to major risk if the stock suddenly performs poorly. If you want to invest in the next market trend, be mindful and allocate a reasonable portion of your funds toward it.

Self-Checklist to Remain Disciplined

Here are some guidelines that can help you remain disciplined in investing. You can use this list to keep yourself accountable.

- Have clear investment goals.
  - Use the SMART methodology to set short-, medium-, and long-term financial goals, like saving for your retirement, buying a house, saving for college (for yourself or your kids), building up an emergency fund, *etc.*
  - Make sure that you have an investment objective for each of your investments. Are they for growth, stability, or income?
- Set thresholds for profit-taking and stop-loss.
  - For profit-taking, decide on a price or percentage gain at which you want to sell an asset or part of

an asset to ensure profit. For example, you can choose to sell 50% of your stock once it gains at least 20% profit.

- For the stop-loss level, you need to also decide on a maximum loss threshold to limit your potential losses. For example, you can decide to sell a stock if it loses 10% of its original purchase value.

- Limit the frequency of trading.
  - Decide on specific periods at which you will check your investments instead of checking them daily (unless your strategy involves short-term trading that needs attention daily). Establish now whether you want to check your investments monthly or quarterly.
  - Have a set rule that allows you to trade only under specific circumstances, like deciding to only rebalance your portfolio when you're busy with a portfolio review and not based on market fluctuations.

- Avoid emotional triggers.
  - If you see something on the news or overhear stock market talk, make a point not to jump onto the train to trade immediately. Don't be moved by your emotions.

- Verify the source of stock tips.
  - Don't allow others to influence your investment decisions by telling you about the newest hot stock. Conduct your own research before you make an investment decision.
  - When taking advice, make sure that it's from a trusted and verified source.

- Diversify across sectors.

- Include assets from various sectors in your portfolio. Avoid putting too much of your capital into a single stock or sector to manage risk.
- Write your investment decisions down.
  - Whenever you make an investment decision, record it in a journal so that you can refer to it. By doing this, you can always go back and recognize patterns of possible impulsive behavior. When we're aware of these, we can make an effort to be more thoughtful in our decision-making the next time.
- Stick to your investment strategy.
  - Don't allow any short-term market moves to change your investment decision. When it's time to make a change, this should be driven by your financial goals and not market fluctuations.

Ignoring Fundamental Analysis

Fundamental analysis involves thoroughly researching a company before you invest. We discussed reviewing financial statements and other metrics in detail in Chapter 2. Going through this analysis gives you a proper picture of whether the investment is right for you and will add any value to your portfolio.

Often, when we let emotions drive our investments, overtrade, or chase hot stocks, we neglect thorough analysis, which increases the risk of making poor investment decisions. When we only rely on market trends, tips, and speculation and ignore this fundamental analysis, we run the risk of filling our portfolio with dangerous stocks that can do a lot of harm.

Here is a quick recap on what to look at when you're analyzing a stock for investment:

- Learn more about the company. Understand their business model, which industry they operate in, analyze their management, etc.
- Examine and evaluate their financial records.
- Study the annual report.
- Consider the company's prospects.
- Calculate the key ratios as discussed in Chapter 2.
- Determine whether they have a competitive advantage and what it is.

Chapter Summary

- We are emotional beings and often make decisions based on our emotions. When it comes to investing, it's best to push our emotions to the side and make decisions based on factual information.
  - The two main emotions we tend to experience when investing are fear and greed. Fear when the market starts going down and greed when it improves.
  - There are three key heuristics to be aware of, namely Gambler's fallacy, overconfidence bias, and the recency effect.
  - To avoid emotional investing, you need to define your goals and time horizon, use the bucketing approach, stick to your investment strategies, and involve a professional.

- Overtrading (consistently buying and selling stocks) is another pitfall that new investors often face.
  - Overtrading can occur due to boredom, greed, over-excitement, and vengeance.
  - You can avoid overtrading by setting some rules, not giving into emotional investing, taking a break, knowing when to stop, and not losing focus on your long-term goals.
- Chasing hot stocks happens when we focus on what is trending instead of choosing stocks based on research.
- The pitfalls commonly occur because we ignore fundamental analysis, which can be avoided by following a strategic and vigorous analysis before investing.

CONCLUSION

We all have to start somewhere. Some start on the golf course by rubbing shoulders with experienced investors, some with a small investment. Your story might begin with this book if it hasn't already. It might be boring, but you need to start with the fundamentals. Successful investors didn't just jump in and invest. They spent time researching and speaking to seasoned investors to gain the knowledge required to take the next step.

Setting up your portfolio is the hardest part, but the hard work doesn't stop there. You need to remain informed and consistently manage your portfolio.

When starting up, you need to decide on an investment strategy. The investment strategy you select must be suitable for your ability to take risks, how comfortable you are with them, and your financial goals. It's pivotal to have a clear investment plan (which involves your strategy) from the beginning to avoid making mistakes or having to start over.

Your investment plan can contain individual brokerage accounts and retirement accounts like traditional IRA or Roth IRA. By investing in an IRA, you can derive additional tax benefits, either tax-deferred or tax-exempt. However, there are limitations to how and when you can access the money in IRAs.

As long as you focus on diversification within your profile, you should be able to build a good base. The asset allocation in your portfolio for diversification should be aligned with your age, risk tolerance, investment goals, and investment objective. When you're ready to start choosing your investments, you need to research the companies properly.

Once you start getting the hang of investing, you can take the next step to analyze companies you are interested in and properly review their financial statements and annual reports. Do the necessary research to ensure that you are making wise investment decisions. If you know what to look for, reviewing a company is a breeze.

These initial investment decisions don't need to be forever. You need to regularly review your portfolio and make the necessary adjustments to capitalize on the investment market as much as possible. However, you must set a time to review and rebalance to avoid being moved by market fluctuations.

The stock market is very volatile, and when we watch our investments and the market too closely, we might resort to emotional investing or overtrading. The market will fluctuate, but if there is anything we can learn from history, it's that the market always has recovered.

As you get older, you'll need to adjust the asset allocation percentages in your portfolio to match your new risk tolerance and remain aligned with your goals while keeping the future (and retirement) in mind. You want to take less risk as you age because you won't have as much time to recover should anything happen. We've seen that even with proper research, mistakes can still be made, and the market will still do its own thing. We can't actually predict what's going to happen, and the only thing you can do is apply strategies to manage the risk of losing.

I hope this book was able to provide a strong base for you to begin your investing journey. To help others discover this resource, please consider leaving a review if you found it useful.

Until next time. Keep learning, stay patient, and let your investments grow along with you.

NEXT STEPS

Building a strong financial foundation is one of the most empowering decisions you can make. These books are designed to help you take charge of your money by teaching the essentials of personal finance. They're excellent tools for developing the skills needed to achieve long-term financial success. Look for these titles on Amazon, or simply scan the barcode to dive in!

Financial Literacy for Young Adults Simplified: Discover How to Manage, Save, and Invest Money to Build a Secure & Independent Future

If you're just beginning your journey into personal finance, this book is the perfect starting point. It discusses budgeting, saving, and investing, presenting them as straightforward, actionable steps. You'll build a strong financial foundation, setting the stage for tackling more advanced concepts in the future.

Financial Literacy for Young Adults Amplified: Prepare for Inflation & Recession, Decide Between Buying or Renting, & Borrow Smarter

Ready to elevate your financial knowledge? This book covers advanced topics in finance, such as inflation and recessions, and offers guidance on key financial decisions, including renting versus buying and responsible debt management. It's designed to help you navigate real-world financial challenges with confidence and make informed choices that shape your future.

Smart Money Habits for Young Adults: to Build Wealth
Avoid Emotional Spending, Impulsive Investments, & Biased Thinking to Build a Secure Financial Future

Want to build better money habits and grow your wealth? Smart Money Habits for Young Adults to Build Wealth dives into the psychological factors behind emotional spending, impulsive investments, and biased thinking. This easy-to-follow guide helps you understand your mindset, make smarter financial choices, and create a secure future.

GLOSSARY

Asset allocation: A portfolio strategy that allocates investments across various asset classes (stocks, bonds, cash) to manage risk and reward according to the investor's objectives, risk profile, and investment horizon.

Asset: Any resource or item of value that can be used to generate income or capital gains.

Balanced portfolio: A portfolio that includes a mix of asset classes to help balance risk and reward. The goal is diversification, which aims to protect the investor against volatility in any single market sector.

Bear market: A market characterized by falling prices, typically a decline of 20% or more in broad stock indices.

Bonds: Debt securities issued by governments or corporations that pay interest over time. They are typically less volatile than stocks and offer more stable returns.

Bull market: Defined by rising or anticipated price increases, often reflected in sustained stock market growth.

Capital gains tax: Profits from selling investments—stocks, real estate, bonds, etc.—are subject to taxes.

Capital gains. You profit from selling assets, including stocks and real estate, if the selling price exceeds the purchase price.

Compound interest: Interest that is calculated not only on the original principal but also on the interest that accumulates over time. This mechanism enables investments to grow at an accelerating rate.

Diversification: A strategy of spreading investments across different assets or sectors to reduce risk.

Diversified portfolio: A portfolio that includes different types of investments (stocks, bonds, real estate, etc.) to reduce the risk of a total loss.

Dividend: Companies often distribute a portion of their earnings to shareholders as dividends, usually in cash or extra shares.

Dollar-cost averaging: By investing a fixed amount at set intervals, this strategy aims to lessen the effects of market ups and downs.

Financial Literacy: The capacity to comprehend and proficiently handle personal finances, encompassing essential principles such as budgeting, investing, and saving.

Intrinsic value: The true value of an asset, found by analysis, not its current market price.

Liquidity: How easy it is to sell an asset without affecting its price.

Portfolio: An individual's collection of investments.

Real Estate Investment Trusts (REITs). Businesses that profit from real estate by owning, running, or providing financial backing. Investors can buy shares in these trusts as a way to invest in real estate without directly owning property.

Return on investment (ROI): A metric to assess how well an investment performs, calculated by comparing the profit or loss against the initial investment.

Risk and return: The concept that higher returns generally come with higher risk. It describes the tradeoff between the potential profit and the possibility of loss associated with an investment.

Risk mitigation: The process of reducing or managing potential investment risks through strategies like diversification, research, and setting limits.

Risk tolerance: The level of fluctuation in investment returns that an individual is prepared to experience in order to achieve their financial objectives.

Risk-return tradeoff: The balance between the risk involved in an investment and the expected return. While higher risk may lead to higher returns, these returns are not guaranteed.

Securities: Tradable financial assets, including stocks, bonds, and options.

Shares: Units of stocks.

Stock exchanges: Platforms or places where stocks are traded, such as the New York Stock Exchange (NYSE).

Stock market: A marketplace where shares of publicly held companies are bought and sold.

Stock: A share in the ownership of a company

Stockbroker: Licensed individuals or firms that act on behalf of others to buy and sell stocks and other securities.

Time horizon: The length of time someone plans to hold an investment before they think they need to access the funds.

Volatility: The degree of variation of an investment's price over time. High volatility means larger price swings, which may indicate higher risk.

REFERENCES

Abraham, S. A. (2024, February 29). *Is dividend investing a good strategy?* Investopedia. https://www.investopedia.com/articles/basics/11/due-dilli gence-on-dividends.asp#toc-the-risks-to-dividends

Akinnibi, F. (2023, March 2). The impact of diversification on portfolio performance: A case study of the 2008 financial crisis. *Cowrywise.* https://cowry wise.com/blog/case-study-of-2008-financial-crisis/

Are you a value investor or a growth investor? (2021, September 8). Protect Financial. https://protectfinancial.ca/2021/09/08/are-you-a-value-investor-or-a-growth-investor/

Ashford, K. (2024, July 30). *The life-changing magic of compound interest.* Forbes Advisor. https://www.forbes.com/advisor/investing/compound-interest/

Avoid the emotional investing trap. (2022, October 4). Charles Schwab. https://www.schwab.com/learn/story/avoid-emotional-investing-trap

Axelton, K. (2023, May 3). How to avoid emotional investing. *Experian.* https://www.experian.com/blogs/ask-experian/how-to-avoid-emotional-investments/

Berger, R., & Curry, B. (2023, November 29). *How diversification works, and why you need it.* Forbes Advisor. https://www.forbes.com/advisor/investing/what-is-diversification/

Bergthold, Z. (2024, February 16). Strategies for minimizing capital gains taxes. *Be Wellthy* Blog. https://www.brightonjones.com/blog/strategies-for-mini mizing-capital-gains-taxes/

Berman, L. (2017, September 11). *Are you a growth investor? What is your investment personality?* Berman's Call. https://www.bermanscall.com/behav ioural-finance/growth-investor-investment-personality/

Berry-Johnson, J. (2021, January 13). Financial statements 101. *Bench.* https://www.bench.co/blog/accounting/financial-statements

Bezek, I. (2024, October 17). *15 best dividend stocks to buy now.* U.S. News & World Report. https://money.usnews.com/investing/articles/best-divi dend-stocks-to-buy-this-year

Bhattacharyya, R. (2024, August 21). *Overtrading.* WallStreetMojo. https://www.wallstreetmojo.com/overtrading/

Bloomenthal, A. (2023, September 10). *How to pick the best dividend stocks.*

Investopedia. https://www.investopedia.com/articles/active-trading/042315/top-dividend-stocks-how-pick-them.asp

Brock, C. (2023, November 10). *5 things to know about asset allocation.* The Motley Fool. https://www.fool.com/retirement/strategies/asset-allocation-by-age/

Brock, C. (2024, September 30). *The value investing strategy.* The Motley Fool. https://www.fool.com/investing/stock-market/types-of-stocks/value-stocks/value-investing-guide/

Buchanan, C. (2023, June 21). *5 steps to review your investment portfolio.* Chase Buchanan. https://chasebuchanan.com/5-steps-to-review-your-investment-portfolio/

Campbell, T., & Yale, A. J. (2024, July 19). *How to start a Roth IRA: A guide for beginners.* Business Insider. https://www.businessinsider.com/personal-finance/investing/how-to-open-ira

CFI Team. (n.d.-a). *Asset allocation.* Corporate Finance Institute. https://corporatefinanceinstitute.com/resources/wealth-management/asset-allocation/

CFI Team. (n.d.-b). *Common vs preferred shares.* Corporate Finance Institute. https://corporatefinanceinstitute.com/resources/equities/common-vs-preferred-shares/

CFI Team. (n.d.-c). *Short-Term vs long-term investors.* Corporate Finance Institute. https://corporatefinanceinstitute.com/resources/career-map/sell-side/capital-markets/short-term-vs-long-term-investors/

CFI Team. (n.d.-d). *Stock exchange.* Corporate Finance Institute. https://corporatefinanceinstitute.com/resources/equities/stock-exchange/

CFI Team. (n.d.-e). *Stock market.* Corporate Finance Institute. https://corporatefinanceinstitute.com/resources/career-map/sell-side/capital-markets/stock-market/

Chen, J. (2022a, April 25). *Overtrading: Definition, causes, types, and ways to avoid.* Investopedia. https://www.investopedia.com/terms/o/overtrading.asp

Chen, J. (2022b, May 27). *Chasing the market: What it is, how it works, pros and cons.* Investopedia. https://www.investopedia.com/terms/c/chasingthemarket.asp

Chen, J. (2023, October 11). *What is asset allocation and why is it important?* Investopedia. https://www.investopedia.com/terms/a/assetallocation.asp

Chen, J. (2024a, May 15). *Risk-return tradeoff: How the investment principle works.* Investopedia. https://www.investopedia.com/terms/r/riskreturntradeoff.asp

Chen, J. (2024b, May 16). *Risk: What it means in investing, how to measure and manage it.* Investopedia. https://www.investopedia.com/terms/r/risk.asp

References

Chen, J. (2024c, July 23). *Capital gains: Definition, rules, taxes, and asset types.* Investopedia. https://www.investopedia.com/terms/c/capitalgain.asp

Chen, J. (2024d, August 9). *Who is Peter Lynch?* Investopedia. https://www.investopedia.com/terms/p/peterlynch.asp

Chen, J. (2024e, October 7). *What is a brokerage account? Definition, how to choose, and types.* Investopedia. https://www.investopedia.com/terms/b/brokerageaccount.asp

Clarance, C. (2023, September 6). *Market volatility, dollar cost averaging and your savings.* North Peace Savings. https://npscu.ca/knowledgebase/market-volatility-dollar-cost-averaging-and-your-savings/

Competitive advantage. (n.d.). Airfocus. https://airfocus.com/glossary/what-is-competitive-advantage/

Cook, D. (2024a, March 10). *2 reasons to buy apple stock like there's no tomorrow.* Yahoo Finance. https://finance.yahoo.com/news/2-reasons-buy-apple-stock-073000374.html

Cook, D. (2024b, May 19). *3 reasons to buy apple stock like there's no tomorrow.* The Motley Fool. https://www.fool.com/investing/2024/05/19/3-reasons-to-buy-apple-like-theres-no-tomorrow/

Davis, C. (2024, March 1). *What is the stock market?* NerdWallet. https://www.nerdwallet.com/article/investing/what-is-the-stock-market

Delossantos, C. (2023). From hype to bust: Investigating the underlying factors of the dot-com bubble and developing regression models for future market predictions. *Open Journal of Business and Management, 11*(5), 2161–2174. https://doi.org/10.4236/ojbm.2023.115119

Desjardins, J. (2019, February 12). *5 lessons about volatility to learn from the history of markets.* Visual Capitalist. https://www.visualcapitalist.com/5-lessons-about-volatility-to-learn-from-the-history-of-markets/

Dobosz, J. (2023, June 8). *10 key financial ratios every investor should know.* Forbes. https://www.forbes.com/sites/investor-hub/article/10-key-financial-ratios-every-investor-should-know/

Dolan, B. (2024, October 8). *Who is Warren Buffet? How did he make his fortune?* Investopedia. https://www.investopedia.com/articles/financial-theory/08/buffetts-road-to-riches.asp

Editorial Team. (2024, March 25). *Market volatility and the triggers of investor behavior.* Howard Capital Management. https://howardcm.com/index.php/2024/03/25/market-volatility-and-the-triggers-of-investor-behavior/

Engelberg, J., & Parsons, C. A. (2016). Worrying about the stock market: Evidence from hospital. *The Journal of Finance. 71*, 1227–1250. https://doi.org/10.1111/jofi.12386

References

Enochson, H. (2022, June 24). *How to identify competitive advantages.* OnStrategy. https://onstrategyhq.com/resources/identify-competitive-advantages/

Fajasy. (2024, July 12). *How to evaluate a company's management team.* StableBread. https://stablebread.com/how-to-evaluate-a-companys-management-team/

Farley, A. (2022, September 30). *Figure out your investment goals.* Investopedia. https://www.investopedia.com/investing/figure-out-your-investment-goals/#toc-how-much-do-you-need-to-save

Fernando, J. (2024a, February 28). *The power of compound interest: Calculations and examples.* Investopedia. https://www.investopedia.com/terms/c/compoundinterest.asp

Fernando, J. (2024b, October 23). *Capital gain tax: What it is, how it works, and current rates.* Investopedia. https://www.investopedia.com/terms/c/capital_gains_tax.asp

Folger, J. (2022, July 20). *5 advantages of investing in your 20s.* Investopedia. https://www.investopedia.com/financial-edge/0212/5-advantages-to-investing-in-your-20s.aspx

Fonville, M. (2024, September 26). *9 crucial components of an investment portfolio review.* Covenant Wealth Advisors. https://www.covenantwealthadvisors.com/post/9-crucial-components-investment-portfolio-review

Frankel, M., & Tretheway, C. (2024, September 19). *How to open a brokerage account: A step-by-step guide.* The Motley Fool. https://www.fool.com/the-ascent/buying-stocks/how-to-open-brokerage-account/

Friedberg, B. A. (2024, January 7). *How to rebalance your portfolio.* Investopedia. https://www.investopedia.com/how-to-rebalance-your-portfolio-7973806

Fundamental analysis: A complete guide. (n.d.). *Winvesta.* https://www.winvesta.in/blog/fundamental-analysis-a-complete-guide

Gadodia, V. (n.d.). *Trading in stock market: Advantages and disadvantages.* My Espresso-Bootcamp. https://www.myespresso.com/bootcamp/module/trading-basics/advantages-disadvantages-of-stock-trading

Gratton, P. (2024, April 12). *What is the stock market and how does it work?* Investopedia. https://www.investopedia.com/terms/s/stockmarket.asp

Haegele, B. (2024, January 12). *Investing vs speculating: What's the difference?* Bankrate. https://www.bankrate.com/investing/investing-vs-speculating/

Hall, J. (2024, March 6). *How to invest in dividend stocks: A guide to dividend investing.* The Motley Fool. https://www.fool.com/investing/stock-market/types-of-stocks/dividend-stocks/how-to-invest-in-dividend-stocks/

Harper, D. R. (2024, May 20). *Forces that move stock prices.* Investopedia. https://www.investopedia.com/articles/basics/04/100804.asp

Hartill, R. (2024, September 4). *How to set your investment goals*. The Motley Fool. https://www.fool.com/investing/how-to-invest/how-to-set-investment-goals/

Hayes, A. (2020, December 30). *Factors to consider when evaluating company management*. Investopedia. https://www.investopedia.com/articles/02/062602.asp

Hayes, A. (2023a, September 1). *Value investing definition, how it works, strategies, risks*. Investopedia. https://www.investopedia.com/terms/v/valueinvesting.asp

Hayes, A. (2023b, December 2). *Defining your basic investing objectives: What to factor in*. Investopedia. https://www.investopedia.com/managing-wealth/basic-investment-objectives/

Hayes, A. (2023c, December 11). *Growth stock: What it is, examples, vs. value stock*. Investopedia. https://www.investopedia.com/terms/g/growthstock.asp

Hayes, A. (2024a, April 17). *Cash flow: What it is, how it works, and how to analyze it*. Investopedia. https://www.investopedia.com/terms/c/cashflow.asp

Hayes, A. (2024b, May 13). *Stocks: What they are, main types, how they differ from bonds*. Investopedia. https://www.investopedia.com/terms/s/stock.asp

Hayes, A. (2024c, May 23). *Dollar-cost averaging (DCA) explained with examples and considerations*. Investopedia. https://www.investopedia.com/terms/d/dollarcostaveraging.asp

Hayes, A. (2024d, September 4). *Revenue definition, formula, calculation, and examples*. Investopedia. https://www.investopedia.com/terms/r/revenue.asp

Hayes, A. (2024e, October 25). *Understanding a traditional IRA vs other retirement accounts*. Investopedia. https://www.investopedia.com/terms/t/traditionalira.asp

Hellwig, B. (2023, May 15). *Know your shareholder rights*. Investopedia. https://www.investopedia.com/investing/know-your-shareholder-rights/

Hicks, C., & Alberstadt, H. (2024, September 27). *Roth IRA: A guide to investing and trading*. USA Today. https://www.usatoday.com/money/blueprint/retirement/roth-ira-investing-and-trading/

Hill, H. (2023, June 13). *How often should I review my investment portfolio?* BentOak Capital. https://bentoakcapital.com/investment-management/how-often-should-i-review-my-investment-portfolio/

History of stock market: Everything to know how it all started. (n.d.). Strike. https://www.strike.money/stock-market/history

HL_Inv. (2024, July 1). *Adjusting your investment strategy as you age*. Highlight

Investment. https://www.highlightinvestment.com/adjusting-your-invest
ment-strategy-as-you-age/

How do investors use financial statements? (2023, January). Accountancy
Cloud. https://accountancycloud.com/blogs/how-do-investors-use-finan
cial-statements

How much is too much cash in your portfolio? (2024). Merrill Lynch. https://www.
ml.com/articles/how-much-is-too-much-cash-in-your-portfolio.html

How to evaluate management quality before buying stocks? (2022, November
7). *ET Money.* https://www.etmoney.com/blog/how-to-evaluate-manage
ment-quality-before-buying-stocks/

How to keep calm during market volatility. (2024, June 27). RBC Brewin Dolphin.
https://www.brewin.co.uk/insights/how-keep-calm-during-market-
volatility

Hwang, I. (2024, February 27). *A brief history of the stock market and stock
exchanges.* SoFi. https://www.sofi.com/learn/content/history-of-the-stock-
market/

Investing basics: Risk. (2024). Finra. https://www.finra.org/investors/investing/
investing-basics/risk

Kagan, J. (2024, January 19). *Who was Benjamin Graham?* Investopedia. https://
www.investopedia.com/terms/b/bengraham.asp

Khan, R. (2023, August 16). *The roller coaster of emotional investing and its impact
on portfolios.* Visual Capitalist. https://www.visualcapitalist.com/sp/roller-
coaster-of-emotional-investing/

Lawler, J. (2023, November 3). *What makes a good dividend stock?* Trading 212.
https://www.trading212.com/learn/dividends/what-makes-a-good-divi
dend-stock

Levy, A. (2024, September 17). *Best growth stocks: Top picks for October 2024.* The
Motley Fool. https://www.fool.com/investing/stock-market/types-of-
stocks/growth-stocks/#toc_large-addressable-markets

Liberto, D. (2024, June 19). *Cash reserves: What they are and how they work.*
Investopedia. https://www.investopedia.com/terms/c/cash-reserves.asp

Malito, A. (2021, June 26). *How Peter Thiel turned $2,000 in a Roth IRA into
$5,000,000,000.* MarketWatch. https://www.marketwatch.com/story/how-
peter-thiel-turned-2-000-in-a-roth-ira-into-5-000-000-000-11624551401

Maranjian, S. (2014, December 4). *Why chasing hot stocks could burn you.* The
Motley Fool. https://www.fool.com/investing/general/2014/12/04/why-
chasing-hot-stocks-could-burn-you.aspx

Market bubbles and volatility. (2023, September 26). Get Smarter about Money.

https://www.getsmarteraboutmoney.ca/learning-path/understanding-risk/market-bubbles-and-volatility/

Marston, R. (2018, April 16). *How retirement strategies should change as you age.* Forbes. https://www.forbes.com/sites/impactpartners/2018/04/16/how-retirement-strategies-should-change-as-you-age/

McBride, G. (2024, January 29). *What is risk tolerance and why is it important?* Bankrate. https://www.bankrate.com/investing/what-is-risk-tolerance/

McCoy, J. (2024, February 20). 7 competitive advantage examples for business success. *BrandWell.* https://brandwell.ai/blog/competitive-advantage-examples/

McWhinney, J. (2021, December 5). *Use dollar-cost averaging to build wealth over time.* Investopedia. https://www.investopedia.com/investing/dollar-cost-averaging-pays/

Mehta, K. (2024, August 21). *Risk return trade off* (A. K. Srivastav, Ed.). WallStreetMojo. https://www.wallstreetmojo.com/risk-return-trade-off/

Mitchell, C. (2022, October 24). *Are you undertrading or overtrading?* Investopedia. https://www.investopedia.com/articles/trading/09/undertrading-over trading-trading-plan.asp

Moreano, G. (2024, March 13). *Rebalancing your portfolio: What that means and how often to do it.* Bankrate. https://www.bankrate.com/investing/portfolio-rebalancing/

Murphy, C. B. (2024, August 4). *Financial statements: List of types and how to read them.* Investopedia. https://www.investopedia.com/terms/f/financial-statements.asp

Nadelle, D. (2024, April 26). *Why Warren Buffett loves compound interest: The "8th wonder of the world"?* Nasdaq. https://www.nasdaq.com/articles/why-warren-buffett-loves-compound-interest:-the-8th-wonder-of-the-world

Napoletano, E. (2023, July 11). *Understanding asset allocation.* Forbes Advisor. https://www.forbes.com/advisor/investing/what-is-asset-allocation/

Nguyen, J. (2024, August 5). *Investing vs. speculating: What's the difference?* Investopedia. https://www.investopedia.com/ask/answers/09/difference-between-investing-speculating.asp

O'Shea, A. (2024a, April 29). *How to invest your IRA* (C. Hutchison, Ed.). NerdWallet. https://www.nerdwallet.com/article/investing/how-to-invest-ira

O'Shea, A. (2024b, April 29). *How to open an IRA in 4 steps* (C. Hutchison, Ed.). NerdWallet. https://www.nerdwallet.com/article/investing/how-and-where-to-open-an-ira

O'Shea, A. (2024c, September 20). *What is a brokerage account? Definition, how to open one.* NerdWallet. https://www.nerdwallet.com/article/investing/what-is-how-to-open-brokerage-account

Peart, K. N. (2021, October 14). *Yale endowment earns 40.2% investment return in fiscal 2021.* Yale News. https://news.yale.edu/2021/10/14/yale-endowment-earns-402-investment-return-fiscal-2021

PenMypaper. (n.d.). A complete guide to Apple's competitive advantage. https://penmypaper.com/knowledge-base/apple-competitive-advantages

Peter, R. (2024, April 9). *The importance of staying informed: Why investors must follow the markets.* Medium. https://medium.com/@rolandpeter656/the-importance-of-staying-informed-why-investors-must-follow-the-markets-2a31a72c84e5

Pinkasovitch, A. (2024, September 23). *Tax-deferred vs. tax-exempt retirement accounts.* Investopedia. https://www.investopedia.com/articles/taxes/11/tax-deferred-tax-exempt.asp

Poke, P. (2024, March 6). *Playing with fire: The dangers of chasing hot trends.* Betashares. https://www.betashares.com.au/insights/dangers-of-chasing-hot-trends/

Prabhu, A. (2023, March 24). The seven types of competitive advantage. *Profit.co.* https://www.profit.co/blog/performance-management-blog/the-seven-types-of-competitive-advantage/

Raje, A. (2024, January 19). *Factors affecting share prices in the stock market.* Kotak Life. https://www.kotaklife.com/insurance-guide/wealth-creation/factors-affecting-stock-markets#

Rapacon, S. (2024, January 10). *7 tips for long-term investing.* Forbes Advisor. https://www.forbes.com/advisor/investing/tips-for-long-term-investing/

Ray Dalio. (2022, October 11). Academy of Achievement. https://achievement.org/achiever/ray-dalio/

Regular investment portfolio review is so important! (n.d.). Austen Morris Associates. https://austenmorris.com/regular-investment-portfolio-review-is-so-important/

Reiff, N. (2024, February 26). *Benefits of holding stocks for the long term.* Investopedia. https://www.investopedia.com/articles/investing/052216/4-benefits-holding-stocks-long-term.asp

Risk tolerance: What is it-and how can I measure it? (n.d.). Merrill. https://www.ml.com/articles/what-is-risk-tolerance.html

Rogers, M. (n.d.). How do investors use financial statements? An inside look. *Zeni.* https://www.zeni.ai/blog/how-do-investors-use-financial-statements

Roth IRA. (n.d.). Charles Schwab. https://www.schwab.com/ira/roth-ira

References

Royal, J. (2024a, April 12). *Dollar-Cost averaging: How to use the strategy to build wealth over time* (M. Barba, Ed.). Bankrate. https://www.bankrate.com/investing/dollar-cost-averaging-what-it-is-avoids-timing-market/

Royal, J. (2024b, April 18). *Should you actively trade in a Roth IRA?* (B. Beers, Ed.). Bankrate. https://www.bankrate.com/retirement/should-you-actively-trade-roth-ira/

Royal, J. (2024c, April 26). *How to open a Roth IRA* (B. Beers, Ed.). Bankrate. https://www.bankrate.com/investing/how-to-open-a-roth-ira/

Royal, J. (2024d, July 15). *10 best long-term investments in October 2024* (B. Beers, Ed.). Bankrate. https://www.bankrate.com/investing/best-long-term-investments/

Sajumon, A. (2021, November 21). *Assessment of management quality before buying stocks.* Fisdom. https://www.fisdom.com/assessment-of-management-quality-before-buying-stocks/

Sajumon, A. (2023, July 1). *Growth stocks - what are they, pros & cons, faqs.* Fisdom. https://www.fisdom.com/growth-stocks/

Seabury, C. (2024, April 30). *Mastering short-term trading.* Investopedia. https://www.investopedia.com/articles/trading/09/short-term-trading.asp

Segal, T. (2021, June 4). *Growth investing: Overview of the investing strategy.* Investopedia. https://www.investopedia.com/terms/g/growthinvesting.asp

Segal, T. (2024a, June 21). *Fundamental analysis: Principles, types, and how to use it.* Investopedia. https://www.investopedia.com/terms/f/fundamentalanalysis.asp

Segal, T. (2024b, July 9). *Profit margin: Definition, types, uses in business and investing.* Investopedia. https://www.investopedia.com/terms/p/profitmargin.asp

Segal, T. (2024c, October 25). *Roth IRA: What it is and how to open one.* Investopedia. https://www.investopedia.com/terms/r/rothira.asp

Sethi, R. (2024, June 14). *Diversified investment portfolios: How to build one (+examples).* I Will Teach You to Be Rich. https://www.iwillteachyoutoberich.com/diversified-portfolio-examples/

Simmons, J. (2024, May 23). *Balancing your portfolio: Asset allocation strategies by age.* Beck Capital Management. https://www.beckcapitalmgmt.com/wealth-management/balancing-your-portfolio-asset-allocation-strategies-by-age/

Singh, M. (2024, August 25). *The 2008 financial crisis explained.* Investopedia. https://www.investopedia.com/articles/economics/09/financial-crisis-review.asp

References

Solá, A. T. (2024, February 6). *Gen Z, millennials want to invest—but many aren't, CNBC/generation lab survey finds. Here are the issues.* CNBC. https://www.cnbc.com/2024/02/06/gen-z-millennials-are-grappling-with-high-cost-of-living.html

Steenbarger, B. (2018, October 14). The psychology of navigating a volatile stock market. *Forbes.* https://www.forbes.com/sites/brettsteenbarger/2018/10/14/the-psychology-of-navigating-a-volatile-stock-market/

Swenson, S. (2024, February 27). *What is competitive advantage?* The Motley Fool. https://www.fool.com/terms/c/competitive-advantage/

The importance of investment recordkeeping. (2024, August 14). Finra. https://www.finra.org/investors/insights/recordkeeping

The Investopedia Team. (2024, June 5). *Intrinsic value defined and how it's determined in investing and business.* Investopedia. https://www.investopedia.com/terms/i/intrinsicvalue.asp

The power of starting early: Why young people should invest when they're ready. (2023, September 19). *Next Gen Personal Finance.* https://www.ngpf.org/blog/investing/the-power-of-starting-early-why-young-people-should-invest-when-theyre-ready/

Three successful stories from real investors. (2024, January 17). AJ Bell. https://www.ajbell.co.uk/articles/investmentarticles/270977/three-successful-investor-stories

Traditional IRA. (n.d.). Charles Schwab. https://www.schwab.com/ira/traditional-ira

Tretina, K. (2024, July 23). *What is the stock market? How does it work?* Forbes Advisor. https://www.forbes.com/advisor/in/investing/what-is-stock-market/

Twin, A. (2022, July 7). *What is risk tolerance, and why does it matter?* Investopedia. https://www.investopedia.com/terms/r/risktolerance.asp#toc-aggressive-risk-tolerance

Twin, A. (2024, June 12). *Competitive advantage definition with types and examples.* Investopedia. https://www.investopedia.com/terms/c/competitive_advantage.asp

Types of investment risk. (2023, September 26). Get Smarter about Money. https://www.getsmarteraboutmoney.ca/learning-path/understanding-risk/types-of-investment-risk/

Understanding stocks. (n.d.). Charles Schwab. https://www.schwab.com/stocks/understand-stocks

Understanding the emotions of investing. (n.d.). Edward Jones. https://www.

edwardjones.ca/ca-en/market-news-insights/personal-finance/investing-strategies/emotional-investing

Vanderburg, D. (2020, March 24). *Market volatility and history's recovery lessons.* MassMutual. https://blog.massmutual.com/retiring-investing/market-volatility-and-history

Vipond, T. (2022, November 26). *Profit margin.* Corporate Finance Institute. https://corporatefinanceinstitute.com/resources/accounting/profit-margin/

WallstreetMojo Team. (2024, August 21). *Investment risk.* WallStreetMojo. https://www.wallstreetmojo.com/investment-risk/

WallStreetMojo Team. (2024, August 21). *Investment* vs *speculation.* WallStreet-Mojo. https://www.wallstreetmojo.com/investment-vs-speculation/

Warnes, B. (2022, June 8). How to read (and analyze) financial statements. *Bench.* https://www.bench.co/blog/accounting/how-to-read-and-analyze-financial-statements

Weltman, B. (2024, September 13). *Capital gains tax rates and potential changes in 2025.* Investopedia. https://www.investopedia.com/taxes/capital-gains-tax-101/#toc-how-to-minimize-or-avoid-capital-gains-tax

What is a brokerage account. (n.d.). Charles Schwab. https://www.schwab.com/brokerage/what-is-a-brokerage-account

Why diversification matters. (2024, September 13). Fidelity. https://www.fidelity.com/learning-center/investment-products/mutual-funds/diversification

Wilkins, G. (2023, October 13). *6 basic financial ratios and what they reveal.* Investopedia. https://www.investopedia.com/financial-edge/0910/6-basic-financial-ratios-and-what-they-tell-you.aspx

Wolf, C. (n.d.). Character traits of successful value investors. *The Investor's Podcast Network.* https://www.theinvestorspodcast.com/blog/character-traits-of-successful-value-investors/

Yochim, D. (2024, August 29). *Stock research: How to do your due diligence in 5 steps.* NerdWallet. https://www.nerdwallet.com/article/investing/how-to-research-stocks

Yochim, D., & Durana, A. (2024, February 1). *4 ways to rebalance your portfolio.* NerdWallet. https://www.nerdwallet.com/article/investing/rebalance-portfolio-strategies

Zucchi, K. (2022, July 5). *How to avoid emotional investing.* Investopedia. https://www.investopedia.com/articles/basics/10/how-to-avoid-emotional-investing.asp

www.ingramcontent.com/pod-product-compliance
Lightning Source LLC
Chambersburg PA
CBHW061021220326
41597CB00016BB/2026